EXPLORING THE GST IN INDIA
...A Comprehensive Analysis

Implementation, Impact
& Future Prospectives

Dr. S. N. CHECHANI
Indirect Tax Expert

Made with ♥ on the Notion Press Platform
www.notionpress.com

"For the Sake of Welfare of the Subject, he (The King Dilip) received taxes from them just as the Sun extracts water in order to render it back a thousand-fold."

Raghuvansha Mahakavyam

With Devine Blessings of
"Shree Tukda Mataji"
Chittorgarh, Rajasthan

Dedicated to My Parents

Late Shree Bapu Lal Ji Chechani

&

Mrs. Raju Devi Chechani

Whose

LOVE, AFFECTION & GUIDANCE

Has provided me

STRENGTH & SUPPORT

To be succeeded in every aspect of

My Life-Journey

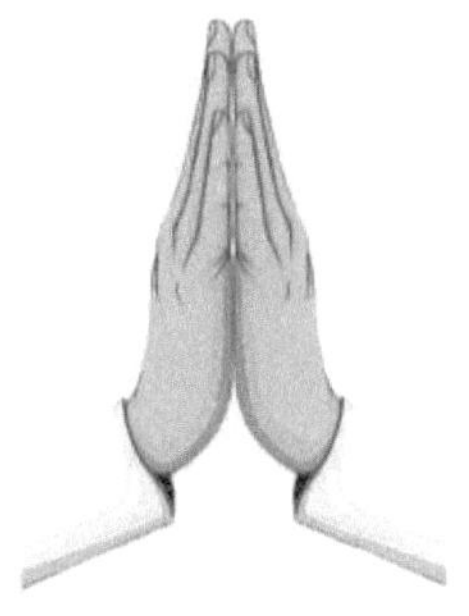

PREFACE

Welcome to the exploration of a critical dimension of contemporary economic landscapes — the Goodsand Services Tax (GST). As we start this journey

through the book "Exploring the Goods and Services Tax (GST): A Comprehensive Analysis of Implementation, Impacts, and Future Perspectives," we focus on the taxation system that has reshaped fiscal policies and economic dynamics.

This book represents a culmination of extensive research, analysis, and a sincere endeavor to unravel the layers of GST, offering readers a comprehensive perspective on its genesis, evolution, and multifaceted impacts.

In an era where global economies are tangled, understanding the complexities of taxation systems is paramount, and GST, with its collaborative and federal structure, stands as a case study of significant importance.

Our exploration begins with the historical evolution of GST, tracing its roots and examining the economic theories that underpin its existence. The formation and functionality of the GST Council, the collaborative decision-making process, and the role of key stakeholders are dissected in subsequent chapters, providing a holistic understanding of the forces shaping GST.

Moving beyond the theoretical framework, we focus on the practicalities — from tax rates and structural frameworks to rule adjustments and the sector-specific implications on small and medium-sized businesses.

The socio-economic impacts on enterprises and individuals add layers to our exploration, offering insights into the broader consequences of GST implementation.

Chapters are dedicated to bridging research gaps, both at the national and regional levels, setting the stage for a more nuanced understanding of GST's effects.

The book takes a turn, with an exclusive study in the small-scale industries sector, examining sectoral variations, traders' perspectives, and the awareness levels among businesses grappling with GST intricacies.

As we progress, the narrative shifts to reflections on the dynamic process of GST implementation, addressing challenges faced by traders, and providing valuable lessons learned.

The concluding chapters offer a forward-looking approach, identifying avenues for future research, formulating a research agenda, and emphasizing the role of academia and industry in shaping the discourse on GST.

This book is not just a scholarly pursuit; it is a practical guide for policymakers, industry professionals, and small traders navigating the evolving landscape of GST. It aspires to contribute to the ongoing dialogue on taxation reforms, offering insights that extend beyond borders and drawing relevance from global experiences.

I invite you to immerse yourself in this comprehensive exploration, hoping that the insights gleaned from these pages contribute to a richer understanding of GST and its implications for the economic layout we navigate today.

Happy reading.

Dr. S. N. Chechani

ACKNOWLEGEMENT

Very primarily, I would like to extend my profound gratitude to **Mr. I. M. Lodha (Renowned Tax Advocate)** who introduced me in the field of Taxation for his active guidance and support, without which it would have been impossible for me to complete this book as the subject matter of this book was very much critical and exhaustive manner.

I am also grateful to my loving wife **Mrs. Archana** & my wonderful children, **Kanishka and Rutwa,** who has provided unending inspiration. In addition, there are my extended family, friends and colleagues, who were of the great imperative resources for me in deliberating over our problems and findings, as well as providing happy distraction to rest mymind.

I must admit that in the preparation of the book I have freely consulted various books and periodicals, authors of which and the authorities of various libraries, I acknowledge my grateful thanks.

I express my apologies that I am not able to mention the names of each and everyone.

Thank you everyone.

Dr. S. N. Chechani

ABOUT THE AUTHOR

Dr. S. N. Chechani, born in 1979, is a distinguished figure in the Indian taxation, law, and advocacy. He has been awarded Doctorate from Bhupals' Noble University, Udaipur. His academic journey also marked by rich qualifications, including a B.Sc., LL.B., and an MBA. Dr. Chechani's academic pursuits are complemented by his  extensive practical experience in the legal field.

Professional Journey:

As an Advocate at the Rajasthan High Court, Dr. Chechani specializes in the field of taxation. His expertise spans a range of tax laws, encompassing GST, VAT, Service Tax, and Income Tax litigation. With over two decades of experience, he has emerged as a seasoned professional in handling direct tax litigation. Acknowledging his proficiency in the legal domain, the Ministry of Legal Affairs, Government of India, awarded Dr. Chechani a certificate of Notary Public. This recognition further attests to his standing in the legal community.

Professional Affiliations:

Dr. Chechani actively contributes to various professional associations, reflecting his commitment to the advancement of the legal and taxation. He holds the position of Secretary at the District Tax Consultant's Association, Chittorgarh, showcasing his leadership and collaborative spirit within the professional community. Additionally, he serves as Secretary at Bharat Vikas Parishad, Nimbahera, contributing to social and community development initiatives.

Academic Contributions:

A true scholar and researcher in matters of indirect taxes, Dr. Chechani has significantly contributed to the academic and professional discourse. He has been a notable speaker and paper writer at numerous national and international conferences, symposiums, and seminars. His research papers find regular publication in leading tax journals, reflecting the depth of his insights and the relevance of his contributions to the field.

Personal Interests:

Beyond the legal arena, Dr. Chechani has a diverse range of interests. He enjoys watching movies, engaging in political and economic debates, and following cricket. This multifaceted approach to life reflects his keen intellect and a well-rounded personality.

Languages:

Fluent in Hindi and English, Dr. Chechani also possesses proficiency in Rajasthani and a comprehension of Gujarati, showcasing his linguistic versatility.

In summary, Dr. S. N. Chechani stands not only as a seasoned Advocate with a specialization in taxation but also as a thought leader, researcher, and active contributor to the legal and academic domains. His comprehensive understanding of tax laws, coupled with a commitment to professional development and community service, solidifies his position as a respected figure in the legal landscape.

TABLE OF CONTENTS

CHAPTER 1

The Genesis of GST

The Goods and Services Tax (GST) stands as a transformative force in taxation, reshaping fiscal policies and economic areas. To understand the contemporary implications of GST, we start our journey through its historical evolution, tracing its roots and examining the economic theories that form the bedrock of its existence.

Historical Evolution:

The roots of GST can be traced back to the early 20th century when discussions on a comprehensive tax system were first initiated. However, it wasn't until the latter half of the century that the idea gained momentum globally. The concept of a unified tax on goods and services emerged as a response to the complexities and inefficiencies of existing tax structures.

India, like many other countries, grappled with a fragmented tax system characterized by cascading effects and multiple layers of taxation. The need for a more streamlined and uniform tax structure became evident, leading to the conceptualization of GST in the Indian context. The journey toward GST in India can be seen as a series of deliberations, committee reports, and policy changes.

The first significant step in the Indian GST journey was the formation of the Kelkar Task Force in 2002, which recommended the introduction of a comprehensive GST.

Subsequently, the Empowered Committee of State Finance Ministers played a pivotal role in shaping the contours of GST in India.

After years of deliberation and negotiation between the Centre and States, the constitutional amendment bill for the introduction of GST was passed in 2016, marking a historic moment in India's taxation history.

Internationally, the evolution of GST has seen diverse models and approaches. From the destination principle in the European Union to the dual GST model in Canada, each country has tailored its GST implementation to suit its economic structure and administrative capabilities. This historical evolution underscores the adaptive nature of GST, with countries customizing the model to align with their economic and administrative landscapes.

Economic Theories and Theoretical Framework:

The genesis of GST is linked to economic theories that advocate for efficiency, equity, and simplicity in taxation.

One of the foundational economic theories underpinning GST is the principle of value-added taxation.

This theory posits that taxes should be levied at each stage of production based on the value added, ensuring that the final consumer bears the ultimate tax burden.

Value-added taxation aligns with the economic efficiency principle by avoiding the cascading effect of taxes.

In traditional tax systems, taxes are levied on the total value of a product at each stage of production, leading to a compounding effect on the overall tax burden. GST, with its emphasis on taxing only the value addition at each stage, mitigates this cascading effect, promoting economic efficiency and minimizing distortions in the production and distribution chains.

Furthermore, GST embodies the principles of neutrality and simplicity in taxation.

By taxing the consumption of goods and services rather than income, GST eliminates distortions in resource allocation and encourages economic agents to make decisions based on market forces.

This neutrality is crucial for fostering a level playing field among businesses and ensuring that resources are allocated efficiently across various sectors of the economy.

The theoretical framework of GST extends beyond economic efficiency to encompass principles of equity and transparency.

GST, by design, aims to be a more equitable tax system as it taxes individuals based on their consumption patterns.

This ensures that those with higher consumption bear a proportionally higher tax burden.

Moreover, the transparent nature of GST, with its clear delineation of tax rates and input tax credits, enhances accountability and reduces opportunities for tax evasion.

The adoption of GST reflects the acknowledgment of these economic theories and the practical application of their principles.

As countries around the world and, in particular, India, embraced GST, they embraced a tax system designed to align with economic efficiency, equity, and simplicity.

In conclusion, the genesis of GST is rooted in a historical evolution marked by the quest for a more efficient and equitable tax system.

The economic theories and theoretical framework underpinning GST emphasize the importance of aligning taxation with economic principles that foster growth, transparency, and fairness.

As we dive deeper into the subsequent chapters, we will untangle the practical implications of these theoretical foundations and examine how they manifest in the contemporary implementation and impacts of GST.

CHAPTER 2

Tracing the GST Council: Shaping the Future of Taxation

The Goods and Services Tax (GST) Council, an important institution in Indian taxation, plays a crucial role in shaping the contours of the GST system.

In this chapter, we will go deep into the composition, functionality, decision-making process, and the authority wielded by the GST Council, while learning about its significant impact on the evolution of GST.

Composition and Functionality:

The GST Council, established under Article 279A of the Indian Constitution, is a unique federal body that brings together representatives from both the Centre and the States. Comprising the Union Finance Minister as the chairperson, the Minister of State for Finance at the Centre, and the Finance Ministers of all the States and Union Territories, the council embodies collaborative federalism in its truest sense.

This composition reflects a consultative and cooperative approach, ensuring that the interests of both the Centre and the States are taken into account. The inclusion of Union Territories with legislatures further extends the council's reach, fostering a comprehensive and inclusive decision-making process.

The functionality of the GST Council is characterized by a deliberative and consensus-driven approach. It serves as a forum for discussions on various issues related to GST, including tax rates, exemptions, and the division of administrative responsibilities. The decisions taken by the council are not only significant for the present but also lay the groundwork for the future evolution of the GST system.

Decision-Making Process:

The decision-making process of the GST Council is marked by a spirit of collaboration and inclusivity. Resolutions within the council are adopted by a three-fourths majority of the weighted votes of members present and voting, where the Centre's vote has a weightage of one-third of the total votes cast, and the votes of all States and Union Territories together have a weightage of two-thirds.

This weighted voting system ensures that major decisions require consensus, preventing unilateral actions that may not align with the collective interests of the diverse Indian states and territories. The emphasis on consensus-building underscores the cooperative federalism embedded in the GST Council's functioning.

The decision-making process extends beyond tax rates and exemptions to cover a spectrum of issues, including the division of tax administration between the Centre and the States, dispute resolution mechanisms, and amendments to the GST law. The deliberations within the council reflect a commitment to addressing the complexities of GST through a consultative and participatory approach.

Authority and Impact on GST Evolution:

The authority vested in the GST Council is a testament to its central role in the evolution of GST. The council's recommendations hold sway not only in the Centre but also across all States and Union Territories. The power to make recommendations on matters affecting the GST system empowers the council to influence the trajectory of GST implementation and administration.

The impact of the GST Council on the evolution of GST is multifaceted. The determination of tax rates, the resolution of disputes, and the continuous refinement of the GST framework all fall within the purview of the council. Its decisions have far-reaching implications for businesses, consumers, and the overall economic landscape of the country.

The authority of the GST Council extends to adapting the GST system to dynamic economic realities. The flexibility embedded in the decision-making process allows the council to respond to changing circumstances, ensuring that the GST framework remains relevant and effective. The council's role in evolving the GST structure reflects a commitment to creating a tax system that is not only efficient but also adaptive to the evolving needs of the Indian economy.

In conclusion, the GST Council stands as a topmost authority in the evolution of the Goods and Services Tax system in India. Its unique composition, collaborative functionality, and authoritative decision-making process underscore the significance of this federal body. As we progress in this exploration, the subsequent chapters will unravel the specific impacts of the GST Council's decisions on tax rates, structural frameworks, and the overall economics.

●●●

CHAPTER 3:

Collaborative Federalism in Action

The implementation and evolution of the Goods and Services Tax (GST) in India stands as a testament to the concept of collaborative federalism, a unique approach that involves active participation and cooperation between the central and state governments.

Let us focus on dynamics of collaborative federalism, exploring the roles of key stakeholders, the decision-making process, and the collaborative efforts that have shaped the GST.

3.1 The Role of Union Finance Minister

At the heart of collaborative federalism in the context of GST is the pivotal role played by the Union Finance Minister. This position holds a central role in overseeing the financial health of the nation and ensuring a harmonious relationship between the central and state governments in matters of taxation.

The Union Finance Minister is responsible for steering the GST Council, a body that brings together representatives from the center and states to collectively decide on crucial aspects of GST implementation. This role extends beyond mere leadership; it involves fostering an environment of consensus and cooperation among diverse stakeholders.

The Council, chaired by the Union Finance Minister, serves as a forum for deliberation, negotiation, and decision-making.

The ministerial leadership ensures that the discussions are guided by a national perspective, taking into account the economic interests of both the central and state governments.

3.2 Delegates from Union Territories and States

Collaborative federalism in the GST framework is manifest in the composition of the GST Council, where delegates from both Union Territories and States come together to collectively shape the course of GST policies. Each state, irrespective of size or economic stature, is given a voice in the decision-making process, promoting inclusivity and representation.

The involvement of Union Territories further reinforces the collaborative spirit, recognizing the diverse economic needs across regions. This inclusive approach ensures that the impact of GST is assessed from a comprehensive, national perspective, taking into account the unique challenges faced by different territories.

The delegates, appointed by their respective governments, bring forth the concerns, insights, and aspirations of their regions to the Council. This diverse representation fosters a robust decision-making process that considers the intricate details of GST implementation and its effects on different states and territories.

3.3 Collaborative Decision-Making

The essence of collaborative federalism is vividly illustrated in the collaborative decision-making processes of the GST Council. Decision-making in the Council is not unilateral; rather, it involves negotiations, discussions, and consensus-building among the representatives.

Crucial aspects such as tax rates, threshold limits, and structural frameworks are subjected to thorough discussions where each representative has a say. This collaborative decision-making is instrumental in addressing the diverse economic landscapes, ensuring that GST policies are not one-size-fits-all but tailored to meet the specific needs of individual states and territories.

The decisions taken in the GST Council reflect a collective vision for the nation's economic future. The collaborative approach ensures that the concerns of both small and large states are considered, fostering a sense of shared responsibility for the success of GST.

Conclusion

In conclusion, collaborative federalism in the context of GST exemplifies the power of collective decision-making and inclusivity. The role of the Union Finance Minister as the leader of the GST Council, the active participation of delegates from Union Territories and States, and the collaborative decision-making processes underscore the commitment to a unified and harmonious approach to taxation.

As we move forward, the exploration of collaborative federalism sets the stage for understanding how this unique model has contributed to the evolution of GST in India. The subsequent chapters will unravel the practical implications of these collaborative efforts, shedding light on how they have shaped the implementation, impacts, and future trajectories of the Goods and Services Tax.

●●●

CHAPTER 4

Setting the Foundation

Tax Rates and Threshold Limitations

Understanding the foundation of the Goods and Services Tax (GST) involves a meticulous examination of the tax rates and threshold limitations that shape this comprehensive taxation system. Let us focus on how tax rates are determined and the threshold limitations set to ensure the equitable application of GST.

1. Tax Rates:

The determination of tax rates under GST is a critical aspect that significantly impacts businesses, consumers, and the overall economic arena. Unlike the complex and multi-tiered tax structures that existed before GST, the system aims for simplicity and uniformity. GST typically encompasses multiple tax slabs, each associated with specific goods and services.

a. Multi-Slab Structure:

One prominent feature is the multi-slab structure, which categorizes goods and services into different tax brackets. These slabs often include standard rates, lower rates for essential commodities, and higher rates for luxury items. The rationale behind this approach is to ensure that essential goods are taxed at a lower rate, providing relief to the common man, while luxury items attract a higher tax.

b. Flexibility and Adjustments:

GST systems also allow for flexibility, with provisions for adjustments based on economic conditions and policy objectives. This adaptability ensures that tax rates can be modified to address specific challenges or changes in the economic landscape. Governments often use this flexibility to stimulate or regulate economic activities.

c. Harmonization Efforts:

In the context of global economic integration, efforts are made to harmonize GST rates, fostering smoother international trade. The alignment of tax rates across jurisdictions reduces trade barriers, promotes competitiveness, and contributes to a more integrated global economy.

2. Threshold Limitations:

Threshold limitations play a crucial role in determining the scope of GST applicability for businesses. These limitations define the turnover below which businesses are exempt from GST, aiming to ease the compliance burden on small enterprises.

a. Small and Medium Enterprises (SMEs):

For small and medium-sized enterprises (SMEs), the GST threshold serves as a protective measure, ensuring that businesses with lower turnovers are not unduly burdened by compliance requirements. This recognition of the varying capacities of businesses contributes to a more inclusive and supportive taxation system.

b. Progressive Thresholds:

Countries implementing GST often adopt progressive threshold structures, where businesses with higher turnovers face the obligation of GST compliance. This approach aligns with the principle of progressive taxation, where larger businesses, capable of contributing more, bear a proportionately higher tax burden.

c. Compliance Simplification:

The establishment of threshold limitations is also linked to the simplification of compliance procedures. Small businesses, exempted from GST or subject to simplified procedures, can focus on their operations without the complexities associated with full-scale GST compliance.

Structural Framework of the GST System

The structural framework of the GST system encompasses the rules, regulations, and administrative mechanisms governing its implementation. Let us provide a comprehensive analysis of the structural elements that form the backbone of GST.

1. Legislative Framework:

The legislative framework is fundamental to the GST system, outlining the legal basis, scope, and applicability of the tax. The enactment of GST laws involves the creation of a robust legal structure that defines the rights and obligations of taxpayers, tax authorities, and other stakeholders.

a. Central and State Legislation:

In federal structures like India, the GST framework involves both central and state legislations. The Central Goods and Services Tax (CGST) and State Goods and Services Tax (SGST) laws coexist, each contributing to the overall legal architecture. The harmonization of these laws is essential for a seamless and unified GST system.

b. Legislative Amendments:

The dynamic nature of economies requires flexibility in the legislative framework. Periodic amendments to GST laws enable governments to respond to emerging challenges, address loopholes, and fine-tune the system for optimal effectiveness.

Legislative agility is crucial for ensuring that the GST framework remains relevant and adaptive.

2. Administrative Machinery:

Efficient administration is paramount for the successful implementation of GST. The establishment of a dedicated administrative machinery involves the creation of tax authorities, dispute resolution mechanisms, and compliance enforcement measures.

a. GST Council:

At the core of the administrative structure is the GST Council, responsible for policy decisions, rate determinations, and resolving inter-state issues. The collaborative nature of the GST Council, involving representatives from both the center and states, ensures a cohesive and cooperative approach to GST governance.

b. Tax Authorities:

The GST system designates tax authorities at both central and state levels. These authorities are entrusted with the assessment, collection, and enforcement of GST. The coordination between central and state tax authorities is vital to prevent overlaps and conflicts in jurisdiction.

3. IT Infrastructure

A robust Information Technology (IT) infrastructure is indispensable for the smooth functioning of the GST system. The adoption of technology facilitates online registration, filing of returns, and real-time monitoring of transactions, reducing manual intervention and enhancing efficiency.

a. GST Network (GSTN):

The establishment of the GST Network (GSTN) is a key component of the IT infrastructure. GSTN acts as the technology backbone, providing a common and shared platform for all stakeholders. This centralized system ensures data integrity, accessibility, and streamlined communication among tax authorities.

b. Digital Compliance:

The digitalization of compliance processes not only expedites administrative functions but also enhances transparency and reduces the scope for tax evasion. Taxpayers benefit from simplified procedures and quicker resolutions of compliance-related matters.

4. Compliance Mechanisms:

A well-defined compliance mechanism ensures that businesses adhere to GST regulations. This includes procedures for registration, filing of returns, audit processes, and anti-evasion measures.

a. Input Tax Credit (ITC) Mechanism:

The GST system incorporates an Input Tax Credit (ITC) mechanism, allowing businesses to offset the tax paid on inputs against the final tax liability. This ensures that taxes are not cascaded through the production and distribution chain, promoting efficiency and preventing tax on tax.

b. Anti-Evasion Measures:

To curb tax evasion, the GST framework includes stringent anti-evasion measures. These may involve data analytics, scrutiny of high-risk transactions, and targeted enforcement actions. The use of technology enhances the effectiveness of these measures.

5. Cross-Border Transactions:

For countries with integrated economies and global trade linkages, the GST system extends to cover cross-border transactions. The implementation of the Integrated Goods and Services Tax (IGST) ensures a seamless taxation mechanism for goods and services moving across state borders.

a. IGST Mechanism:

The IGST mechanism simplifies the taxation of inter-state transactions by consolidating taxes at the central level. This avoids complexities associated with multiple state taxes, promoting ease of doing business and fostering economic integration.

6. Education and Awareness Programs:

A well-informed taxpayer base is crucial for the success of any taxation system. Education and awareness programs play a pivotal role in familiarizing businesses and individuals with the nuances of GST, ensuring voluntary compliance and reducing inadvertent errors.

a. Training Initiatives:

Governments and tax authorities conduct training initiatives to educate taxpayers about GST procedures, compliance requirements, and the benefits of the system. These initiatives contribute to a culture of informed and responsible tax practices.

Conclusion:

In conclusion, Chapter 4: Setting the Foundation, has focused on the pivotal elements that constitute the bedrock of the Goods and Services Tax system. From the intricacies of tax rates and threshold limitations to the nuanced structural framework encompassing legislative, administrative, IT, compliance, and educational aspects, this chapter provides a comprehensive understanding of how GST is implemented and governed. The foundation laid by tax rates and threshold limitations, coupled with an efficient structural framework, ensures the equitable application of GST and sets the stage for subsequent chapters to explore the multifaceted impacts and future trajectories of this transformative taxation system.

CHAPTER 5

The Impact of Council Decisions

Rule and Rate Adjustments

The Goods and Services Tax (GST) system is not static; it evolves dynamically based on the decisions made by the GST Council. Let us focus on impact of the council's decisions, focusing on rule and rate adjustments, and traces the evolutionary journey of the GST system.

1. Rule Adjustments:

The operational nuances of the GST system are governed by a set of rules that outline procedures, compliance requirements, and mechanisms for dispute resolution. The GST Council plays a pivotal role in adjusting these rules to enhance the efficiency and effectiveness of the taxation system.

a. Adapting to Economic Realities:

One of the key functions of the GST Council is to adapt the rules to changing economic realities. Economic shifts, market dynamics, and global influences necessitate continuous adjustments to ensure that the rules remain relevant and responsive. The council's ability to swiftly adapt demonstrates the agility required in an economic landscape.

b. Addressing Implementation Challenges:

As the GST system unfolds, challenges in implementation may surface. The council, through its decisions, addresses these challenges by refining and amending rules. This iterative process of adjustment is crucial for minimizing friction in the system and ensuring a smooth experience for businesses and taxpayers.

c. Simplifying Compliance:

Rule adjustments often include measures aimed at simplifying compliance. The GST system strives to be taxpayer-friendly, and the council's decisions to streamline processes and reduce complexities contribute to this goal. Simplified compliance mechanisms foster better tax adherence and facilitate a positive taxpayer experience.

2. Rate Adjustments:

The GST Council holds the authority to revise tax rates, a power that significantly influences consumer behavior, business strategies, and government revenues. Rate adjustments are carefully considered to strike a balance between revenue generation and economic stimulation.

a. Economic Stimulus:

In times of economic downturn or stagnation, the GST Council may opt for rate reductions to stimulate spending. Lower tax rates on certain goods and services encourage consumer spending, promote investments, and provide businesses with the breathing room needed during challenging economic phases.

b. Revenue Considerations:

Conversely, rate adjustments are also made with revenue considerations in mind. The council must strike a delicate balance between providing economic stimulus and maintaining a steady inflow of revenue. Prudent decisions on rate adjustments reflect the council's commitment to fiscal responsibility.

c. Sector-Specific Considerations:

The impact of rate adjustments is not uniform across all sectors. The council considers sector-specific nuances, ensuring that rates align with the characteristics and demands of each industry. This targeted approach contributes to a balanced economic ecosystem.

Evolution of the GST System

The GST system, as we know it today, has undergone a remarkable evolution since its inception. The decisions made by the GST Council have played a pivotal role in shaping this transformative journey.

1. Early Challenges and Revisions:

The initial implementation of GST was not without challenges. Recognizing the practical difficulties faced by businesses, the GST Council made early decisions to revise and refine the system. These revisions were instrumental in addressing teething issues and laying the groundwork for a more robust and responsive GST framework.

2. Introduction of Anti-Profiteering Measures:

In response to concerns about businesses not passing on the benefits of reduced tax rates to consumers, the GST Council introduced anti-profiteering measures. These decisions aimed to ensure that the benefits of rate reductions were effectively transferred to end consumers, fostering transparency and ethical business practices.

3. Shift Towards Simplification:

The evolution of the GST system has seen a consistent shift towards simplification. The council's decisions to simplify return filing procedures, introduce e-invoicing, and leverage technology reflect a commitment to creating a user-friendly and efficient taxation ecosystem. These steps not only reduce the compliance burden on businesses but also enhance the overall ease of doing business.

4. Expansion of the Tax Base:

To broaden the tax base and include a wider range of economic activities, the GST Council has periodically expanded the scope of the GST system. Decisions to bring previously unregulated sectors into the GST ambit demonstrate the council's commitment to creating a more comprehensive and inclusive tax framework.

5. International Alignment and Best Practices:

The GST system has evolved not only in response to domestic considerations but also in alignment with international best practices. The council's decisions to adopt globally accepted norms, especially in areas such as input tax credit and anti-evasion measures, position the Indian GST system on par with international standards.

6. Embracing Technology for Transparency:

A significant facet of the GST system's evolution has been the embrace of technology for transparency and efficiency. The introduction of the GSTN, e-way bills, and digital compliance mechanisms are outcomes of the council's decisions to leverage technology. These advancements not only streamline processes but also contribute to reducing tax evasion and promoting accountability.

7. Sector-Specific Reforms:

The GST Council has demonstrated a nuanced understanding of diverse sectors, leading to sector-specific reforms. Decisions to tailor tax rates and compliance requirements to the unique characteristics of industries contribute to a more equitable and responsive taxation system.

8. Future Preparedness:

The evolutionary journey of the GST system is an ongoing process. The council's decisions are not just reactive but also forward-looking, anticipating future challenges and opportunities. This proactive approach positions the GST system as a dynamic and adaptable framework capable of navigating the uncertainties of the future.

Conclusion:

Chapter 5, "The Impact of Council Decisions," illuminates the profound influence wielded by the GST Council in shaping the destiny of the Goods and Services Tax system. The adjustments made to rules and rates reflect a system that is responsive to economic realities, implementation challenges, and the needs of diverse sectors. The evolution of the GST system showcases a commitment to simplification, transparency, and future preparedness. As we navigate GST, the decisions of the council stand as guideposts, steering the system towards a more equitable, efficient, and resilient future. I invite readers to have a deep dive into the dynamic realm of GST governance, where every council decision leaves an indelible mark on the trajectory of the nation's taxation landscape.

CHAPTER 6

Sector-Specific Focus -
The Impact on Small and Medium-Sized Businesses (SMEs) and Diverse Areas of Taxation

In GST implementation, Chapter 6 serves as an important exploration into the sector-specific nuances, with a keen focus on the effects rippling through Small and Medium-Sized Businesses (SMEs) and the broader implications on diverse areas of taxation. Let us discuss how GST, with its transformative intent, intersects with the fabric of SMEs and resonates across various facets of the taxation landscape.

6.1 Examining Effects on Small and Medium-Sized Businesses (SMEs)

Small and Medium-Sized Businesses (SMEs) form the backbone of many economies, contributing significantly to employment and economic growth. Let us dissect how the implementation of GST has influenced these enterprises, both positively and with challenges to navigate.

GST brought about a paradigm shift in the taxation structure, replacing the complex web of indirect taxes. For SMEs, this shift implied a more straightforward tax regime, reducing the cascading effect of taxes, and fostering a unified market. However, the initial transition posed operational challenges for SMEs unfamiliar with the new system.

One notable impact on SMEs is the compliance burden. Let us evaluate how the introduction of GST compliance mechanisms, including regular return filings, impacted the operational efficiency of SMEs. The digital interface required for GST compliance also led to a technological learning curve, potentially posing challenges for businesses with limited resources.

Furthermore, we will explore the effects on SMEs in terms of market dynamics. The unified tax structure facilitated smoother interstate transactions, enabling SMEs to expand their market reach. However, variations in tax rates across states introduced complexities that SMEs had to adeptly navigate.

6.2 Implications on Diverse Areas of Taxation

Beyond the sphere of SMEs, let us scrutinize the implications of GST on diverse areas of taxation. The shift to GST marked not only a change in the tax structure but also brought forth implications for direct and indirect taxes, impacting businesses, consumers, and the government alike.

6.2.1 Direct Taxes and GST

Let us dissect the interplay between direct taxes and GST, shedding light on how the shift influenced income tax structures and the overall fiscal landscape. The removal of cascading effects under GST influenced profit margins and, subsequently, the calculation of income tax for businesses. This relationship is analyzed to understand the broader implications on direct taxation.

6.2.2 Indirect Taxes and GST

For indirect taxes, the implementation of GST replaced a plethora of levies with a unified tax structure. The chapter examines the repercussions of this transition on goods and services, evaluating the impact on prices, consumption patterns, and overall economic activities. Insights are drawn on how GST altered the dynamics of excise duties, service tax, and other indirect taxes, shaping a new landscape for businesses and consumers.

6.2.3 Cross-Border Transactions and International Taxation

The global nature of many businesses necessitates an examination of how GST impacts cross-border transactions and international taxation. Let us navigate through the complexities of GST in the context of import-export dynamics, assessing its implications on customs duties, international trade agreements, and the competitiveness of businesses in the global arena.

In conclusion, we provided a comprehensive analysis of the sector-specific ramifications of GST, offering insights into its effects on SMEs and diverse areas of taxation. We have equipped you with a nuanced understanding of how GST reshapes the economic landscape at both micro and macro levels.

CHAPTER 7

Beyond Economics -
Socio-Economic Impacts of GST on Enterprises and Individuals

In Goods and Services Tax (GST) implementation, Chapter 7 transcends the conventional boundaries of economic analysis, focusing on the socio-economic impacts that GST casts on both enterprises and individuals. Let us start a holistic exploration, evaluating the ripple effects that GST initiates beyond economics, shaping the societal and individual dimensions.

7.1 Evaluating Socio-Economic Impacts

As GST interweaves with the fabric of society, understanding its socio-economic impacts becomes imperative. Let us navigate through the multifaceted consequences that GST unfolds, scrutinizing its effects on various strata of society.

7.1.1 Employment Dynamics

One of the most important aspects is the impact of GST on employment dynamics. The unified tax structure aims to streamline processes and foster a more transparent business environment. However, we critically evaluate whether the transitional challenges and compliance intricacies under GST may have inadvertently affected job creation, particularly in sectors sensitive to taxation changes.

7.1.2 Social Equity and Inclusivity

The socio-economic lens widens to examine the implications of GST on social equity and inclusivity. By analyzing how the tax reform affects different sectors, shed light on whether GST has contributed to a more inclusive economic landscape or if it has inadvertently created disparities. Insights into the socio-economic fabric guide policymakers in crafting measures that promote fairness and equitable growth.

7.1.3 Consumer Behavior and Spending Patterns

Study of the shifts in consumer behavior and spending patterns induced by GST is important. With the restructuring of tax rates on various goods and services, the socio-economic impacts resonate at the individual level. Understanding how GST influences consumer choices and expenditure provides a nuanced understanding of its broader societal implications.

7.2 Effects on Enterprises and Individuals

7.2.1 Operational Dynamics of Enterprises

For enterprises, adapting to the GST framework involves a paradigm shift in operational dynamics. This section scrutinizes how businesses, both large corporations and small enterprises, navigate through the challenges and opportunities presented by GST. From changes in supply chain management to modifications in pricing strategies, let us find the ways in which GST shapes the operational landscape of enterprises.

7.2.2 Compliance Burden and Technological Adoption

A critical facet explored is the compliance burden imposed by GST on enterprises. The transition to a digitalized taxation system necessitates technological adoption and adherence to stringent compliance protocols. We need to evaluate how enterprises, especially small and medium-sized businesses, cope with these challenges. Insights into technological adoption, digital literacy, and the efficacy of compliance mechanisms provide a comprehensive understanding of the socio-economic challenges faced by enterprises.

7.2.3 Impact on Individual Taxpayers

At the individual level, the socio-economic impacts of GST extend to personal finances. Changes in tax rates, the introduction of new tax categories, and alterations in exemption thresholds collectively influence the financial landscape of individual taxpayers. We must find out how GST aligns with individual financial goals, exploring whether it acts as a catalyst for savings, investments, or alters consumption patterns.

In conclusion, we have unfurled the current socio-economic impacts woven by the implementation of GST. By traversing beyond the economic facets, the chapter sheds light on the intricate interplay between taxation reforms and societal dimensions. Its insights serve as a compass for policymakers, businesses, and individuals alike, navigating the transformative journey initiated by GST and sculpting a socio-economic landscape that aligns with principles of fairness, inclusivity, and economic vitality.

●●●

CHAPTER 8

Understanding the Complexity

Impacts on the Overarching Economy

In economic systems, the Goods and Services Tax (GST) has emerged as a transformative force, promising simplification while bringing with it complexities. Let us focus on the GST's impact on the overarching economy, unraveling the multifaceted consequences that ripple through various sectors and layers of society.

The Ripple Effect on Economic Dynamics

As the GST framework influences the entire supply chain, its implementation triggers a ripple effect across industries, altering economic dynamics. From manufacturers to consumers, every participant in the economic ecosystem experiences the impact of this tax reform. Let us begin by tracing these ripples, examining how changes in taxation resonate through production, distribution, and consumption channels.

1. **Production Dynamics:**

-   **Cost Structures:** The restructuring of tax rates under GST inevitably affects the cost structures for manufacturers. Let us dissect these alterations, exploring how they influence production volumes, pricing strategies, and ultimately, the competitiveness of businesses.

-   **Supply Chain Efficiency:** GST aims to streamline the supply chain, but achieving this requires adjustments. Let us navigate the complexities of supply chain transformations, identifying challenges and opportunities for businesses.

2. Distribution Networks:

- **Interstate Transactions:** With the introduction of Integrated GST (IGST), the dynamics of interstate transactions have undergone significant shifts. Let us analyze how these changes impact distribution networks, exploring logistical challenges and the adaptability of businesses.

3. Consumer Behavior:

- **Pricing and Affordability:** GST directly influences the pricing of goods and services. Let us investigate how changes in tax rates translate into shifts in consumer behavior, with a focus on purchasing patterns, brand loyalty, and overall market demand.

Navigating the Nuances of GST Implementation

While the overarching impact on the economy is substantial, the nuances of GST implementation are equally critical to comprehend. Let us dissect the challenges faced by businesses, policymakers, and tax authorities in navigating the complexities inherent in GST.

1. Compliance Challenges:

- **Transition Period Challenges:** The initial implementation phase often brings about disruptions as businesses adapt to new compliance requirements. Let us explore the challenges faced during this transitional period and how businesses cope with compliance adjustments.

2. Technology Integration:

- **Digital Transformation:** GST is not merely a tax reform; it necessitates a digital transformation in how businesses operate. Let us elucidate the challenges and opportunities arising from the integration of technology into taxation processes, shedding light on the evolving landscape of e-filing, online documentation, and real-time reporting.

3. **Small and Medium-Sized Enterprises (SMEs):**

- ****Adaptation Strategies:**** SMEs often face unique challenges in adapting to the GST framework. The chapter analyzes the nuanced strategies employed by these enterprises to navigate compliance hurdles, cash flow management, and the competitive landscape.

4. **Governmental Responses:**

- **Policy Adjustments:** Governments play a pivotal role in shaping the GST landscape. Let us evaluate how governments respond to challenges by adjusting policies, tax rates, and procedural frameworks to ensure the smooth functioning of the GST system.

Implications for Ongoing Economic Dialogue

The chapter culminates by reflecting on the broader implications of GST on ongoing economic dialogue. It considers how the complexities unravelled in earlier sections contribute to ongoing policy discussions, shape economic reforms, and influence the discourse surrounding taxation.

1. **Policy Development:**

- **Iterative Policy Refinement:** GST is not a static system but an evolving one. This section discusses how ongoing economic dialogue necessitates iterative policy refinement, considering feedback from businesses, consumers, and experts. It explores the role of policymakers in fine-tuning the GST framework to address emerging challenges.

2. **Broader Discourse on Tax Reforms:**

- **Influence on Global Tax Trends:** Let us examine how the complexities of GST implementation contribute to the broader discourse on global tax trends. By drawing comparisons with international practices, it highlights the global implications of India's tax reforms, positioning GST as a key player in the worldwide conversation on taxation.

Conclusion and Limitations

As Chapter 8 draws to a close, it synthesizes the unraveling complexities of GST's impact on the overarching economy. It acknowledges the transformative power of GST, accentuating its role in shaping economic dynamics. However, the chapter also recognizes its limitations, emphasizing that understanding the full spectrum of GST's impact requires continual observation, research, and adaptability to an ever-evolving economic landscape. This chapter serves as a crucial exploration into the heart of the GST complexities, laying the groundwork for subsequent discussions on policy development, economic shifts, and the future trajectory of taxation in India.

CHAPTER 9

Bridging Research Gaps

Analysis of Prior Research

The journey to a comprehensive understanding of the Goods and Services Tax (GST) involves traversing the landscape of prior research. Let us start a critical analysis of existing literature, aiming to bridge research gaps and provide a solid foundation for the exploration of GST. By focusing on the troves of scholarly works, let us seek to identify the threads connecting disparate studies and the areas that require further exploration.

Prior Studies

Let us initiate with a meticulous review of prior research on GST, dissecting academic papers, reports, and case studies. It systematically categorizes the themes that have dominated the existing discourse and identifies the gaps that continue to challenge the depth of our understanding.

1. **Taxation Models and Theories:**

-   **Historical Perspectives:** An exploration of the evolution of taxation models and theories underpins this section. Let us critically evaluate how historical perspectives influence the current understanding of GST, acknowledging the symbiotic relationship between past tax systems and contemporary reforms.

2. **Impact on Businesses:**

-   **Micro and Macro Perspectives:** Existing research often focuses on either micro or macro perspectives when examining the impact of GST on businesses. This part of the chapter scrutinizes the methodologies employed in prior studies, offering insights into the complexities of balancing detailed case studies with broader economic implications.

3. Consumer Behavior and Market Dynamics:

- **Pricing and Purchasing Patterns:** A critical analysis of how consumer behavior and market dynamics are portrayed in prior research forms a key element of this section. Let us assess whether the existing literature adequately captures the nuanced shifts in consumer preferences and the intricacies of market responsiveness to GST changes.

4. Governmental Policies and Responses:

- **Policy Evaluation:** Let us explore how prior research evaluates governmental policies and responses to challenges posed by GST implementation. It examines whether existing studies offer a holistic evaluation of policy effectiveness or focus on specific facets, such as tax rate adjustments or compliance procedures.

National vs. Regional Perspective

Let us transcend the boundaries of individual studies, widening the lens to scrutinize the interplay between national and regional perspectives in GST research. It dissects how the unique economic, cultural, and social contexts of different regions within India contribute to the overall understanding of GST dynamics.

1. National-Level Insights:

- **Uniformity vs. Diversity:** Analyzing research conducted at the national level, the chapter questions whether the quest for uniformity in GST implementation inadvertently overshadows the diverse economic landscapes of different states. It considers how national-level studies address or overlook regional variations in economic structures and taxation needs.

2. **Regional Nuances:**

- **Economic Disparities:** Let us focus on the regional nuances of GST, exploring how economic disparities impact the applicability and effectiveness of the tax system. It raises questions about the adequacy of national-level policies in addressing the unique challenges faced by specific regions, especially those with distinct economic structures and developmental trajectories.

3. **Cultural and Social Dynamics:**

- **Social Implications of GST:** Beyond economic considerations, let us navigate the cultural and social dynamics influencing GST implementation. It examines whether prior research adequately incorporates the diverse sociocultural fabric of different regions, considering factors such as consumer behavior, business practices, and societal expectations.

4. **Policy Implications:**

- **Tailoring Policies to Regions:** Let us conclude this section by discussing the policy implications of national vs. regional perspectives. It contemplates whether policymakers should adopt a more tailored approach, recognizing the need for region-specific policies that align with the unique challenges and opportunities presented by GST in diverse geographical contexts.

Closing the Gap: A Call to Action

Let us focus on the findings of the analysis, emphasizing the urgency of bridging research gaps in the GST landscape. Let us serve as a rallying cry for future researchers, urging them to transcend traditional boundaries and adopt a holistic approach that considers the intricate interplay between national and regional dynamics.

1. Interdisciplinary Collaboration:

- **Beyond Economic Studies:** Let us advocate for interdisciplinary collaboration, encouraging researchers to go beyond traditional economic studies. A comprehensive understanding of GST necessitates collaboration with experts in sociology, cultural studies, and regional economics.

2. Longitudinal Studies:

- **Evolving Perspectives:** Recognizing the dynamic nature of GST implementation, let us propose the adoption of longitudinal studies. Such studies are essential to capture evolving perspectives, allowing researchers to trace the impact of GST over time and adapt their analyses to changing economic and social landscapes.

3. Regional Case Studies:

- **In-Depth Regional Analyses:** Let us call for in-depth regional case studies, advocating for research that dives into the specific challenges faced by different states and territories. Let us emphasize the need for nuanced analyses that consider the unique economic, cultural, and social contexts shaping GST dynamics at the regional level.

4. Policy Recommendations:

- **Tailored Policy Recommendations:** In the final sections, the chapter offers preliminary policy recommendations based on the research gaps identified. It underscores the importance of tailoring policies to specific regions, advocating for a more adaptive and context-sensitive approach to GST implementation.

In essence, Chapter 9 stands as a critical juncture in the exploration of GST, urging researchers, policymakers, and practitioners to build on the foundations laid by prior studies. By bridging research gaps and embracing a holistic understanding that incorporates national and regional perspectives, this chapter paves the way for a more nuanced and comprehensive dialogue on the transformative impact of GST in India.

CHAPTER 10

Focused Examination

Exclusive Study within the Small Scale Industries Sector

In Goods and Services Tax (GST) implementation, let us undertake a focused examination, directing its lens towards the crucial and often nuanced realm of Small Scale Industries (SSI). This exclusive study within the SSI sector aims to unravel the unique challenges, opportunities, and dynamics that this segment encounters in the labyrinth of GST, providing valuable insights for policymakers, researchers, and stakeholders alike.

Understanding the Small Scale Industries Landscape

Let us begin by setting the stage, offering a comprehensive understanding of the Small Scale Industries sector. And delve into the diverse array of businesses encapsulated within this category, from local enterprises to micro-entrepreneurs, each contributing distinctively to the economic fabric of the nation.

1. Microeconomic Significance:

- **Employment Generation:** The SSI sector plays a pivotal role in employment generation, often serving as a lifeline for local communities. Let us explore how GST impacts job creation, wage structures, and the overall economic well-being of individuals employed within SSIs.

2. Entrepreneurial Diversity:

- **Variety of Enterprises:** SSIs span a spectrum of industries, ranging from manufacturing to service-oriented ventures. Let us provide an overview of this diversity, acknowledging that a one-size-fits-all approach to GST might overlook the varied needs and challenges faced by different types of SSI enterprises.

Challenges and Opportunities in GST Implementation

Having laid the groundwork, the chapter moves into a meticulous examination of the challenges and opportunities arising from the implementation of GST within the Small Scale Industries sector.

1. Compliance Burden:

- **Navigating Complex Procedures:** For small businesses with limited resources, the compliance burden of GST can be particularly challenging. Let us dissect the procedures involved in GST compliance, shedding light on how SSIs navigate the complexities of filing returns, maintaining records, and adhering to regulatory requirements.

2. Impact on Cash Flow:

- **Cash Flow Management:** One of the critical challenges for SSIs lies in effectively managing cash flows amidst the fluctuations introduced by GST. Let us explore how the timing of tax payments, input tax credit mechanisms, and refund processes impact the liquidity of small-scale enterprises.

3. Technological Adaptation:

- **Digital Transformation:** GST mandates a significant shift towards digital transactions and record-keeping. Let us examine how SSIs, often operating on a smaller scale, cope with the digital transformation necessitated by GST implementation. It addresses issues related to technology adoption, digital literacy, and the cost implications of such transitions.

4. Access to Credit:

- **Financial Inclusion Challenges:** Access to credit is vital for the growth of SSIs. The chapter probes into how GST affects the credit landscape for small-scale enterprises, exploring the challenges they face in securing loans and financial support.

5. Competitive Landscape:

- **Market Dynamics:** GST has the potential to alter the competitive landscape for SSIs. Let us analyze how changes in tax structures, input costs, and market dynamics influence the competitiveness of small-scale businesses, both locally and in the broader market.

Policy Interventions and Recommendations

Recognizing the unique challenges faced by SSIs, the chapter segues into a discussion on potential policy interventions and recommendations aimed at alleviating these challenges and enhancing the growth prospects of the sector.

1. Simplifying Compliance Processes:

- **Tailored Compliance Measures:** The development of simplified and tailored compliance processes for SSIs is advocated. Let us explore how streamlined procedures, digital tools, and assistance programs can alleviate the compliance burden on small-scale enterprises.

2. Financial Support Mechanisms:

- **Enhancing Access to Credit:** Policymakers are urged to explore mechanisms that enhance financial inclusion for SSIs. Let us discuss potential strategies to improve access to credit, including targeted lending programs, financial literacy initiatives, and collaborations with financial institutions.

3. **Technology Adoption Initiatives:**

- **Promoting Digital Literacy:** Recognizing the importance of technology in GST compliance, let us suggest initiatives to promote digital literacy among small-scale entrepreneurs. Let us explore the role of government-sponsored training programs, partnerships with tech companies, and incentives for adopting digital tools.

4. **Customized Education and Awareness Programs:**

- Tailored Training Programs: Let us emphasize the need for customized education and awareness programs. Let us focus on the potential impact of targeted workshops, seminars, and campaigns designed to equip SSIs with the knowledge and skills necessary for successful GST adaptation.

Navigating the Future: Insights for Stakeholders

As the chapter draws to a close, it synthesizes the findings of the focused examination within the Small Scale Industries sector, offering insights for various stakeholders.

1. **Governmental Agencies:**

- **Informed Policymaking:** Policymakers are encouraged to leverage the insights garnered from this focused examination to inform future policy decisions. Let us emphasize the importance of a nuanced and context-aware approach to policymaking that considers the unique needs of SSIs.

2. **Industry Associations:**

- **Advocacy and Support:** Industry associations play a crucial role in advocating for the interests of SSIs. Let us discuss how these organizations can leverage the findings to strengthen their advocacy efforts, providing targeted support and resources to small-scale enterprises.

3.   Researchers and Academia:

-   **Future Research Avenues:** For researchers and academia, let us identify future research avenues within the Small Scale Industries sector. It calls for continued exploration into the evolving dynamics of GST implementation, the long-term impact on SSIs, and the effectiveness of policy interventions.

Conclusion: A Holistic Perspective

In conclusion, Chapter 10 offers a holistic perspective on GST implementation within the Small Scale Industries sector. By unraveling the challenges, opportunities, and policy recommendations, this focused examination contributes to the broader dialogue on fostering a business-friendly environment for small-scale enterprises. As GST continues to evolve, understanding the unique dynamics of the Small Scale Industries sector becomes imperative for sustainable economic growth and inclusive development.

●●●

CHAPTER 11

Addressing Sectoral Variations

In Goods and Services Tax (GST) implementation, this exploration takes a focused lens to examine sectoral variations, with a particular emphasis on small-scale industries. Titled "Addressing Sectoral Variations," it unfolds as a comprehensive journey into the nuances and intricacies that define the impact of GST on small-scale industries. The aim is to provide readers with a deeper understanding of the challenges, opportunities, and unique dynamics that characterize this vital sector of the economy.

Comprehensive Insights into Small-Scale Industries:

Unveiling the Small-Scale Industries:

To comprehend the implications of GST on small-scale industries, it is imperative to first unravel the fabric of these enterprises. Small-scale industries, often the backbone of many economies, contribute significantly to employment generation, regional development, and fostering entrepreneurship. This exploration delves into the specific characteristics that differentiate small-scale industries from their larger counterparts, recognizing their resilience, adaptability, and role in the socio-economic landscape.

Navigating through Sectoral Variations:

Let us navigate through the diverse small-scale industries, ranging from manufacturing to service-oriented enterprises. By adopting a sector-specific focus, the aim is to capture the unique challenges faced by each sub-sector and how GST resonates differently within these varied contexts. For instance, manufacturing small-scale industries may grapple with supply chain complexities, while service-oriented enterprises might face distinct compliance challenges.

Quantitative and Qualitative Analysis:

To provide a holistic view, both quantitative and qualitative analyses are employed. Quantitatively, statistical data is scrutinized to measure the economic shifts triggered by GST implementation in small-scale industries. Qualitatively, in-depth interviews, case studies, and surveys are conducted to capture the lived experiences of entrepreneurs, shedding light on the day-to-day operational challenges and strategic adaptations.

Sector-Specific Implications:

Beyond a broad-strokes analysis, this exploration meticulously explores the sector-specific implications of GST. This includes evaluating how tax rates impact cost structures, understanding the compliance burden on small-scale enterprises, and discerning the influence of GST on market dynamics. The aim is to equip policymakers, industry stakeholders, and researchers with actionable insights to tailor policies and strategies that cater specifically to the needs of small-scale industries.

Bridging Gaps in Sector-Specific Research:

Identifying Research Gaps:

Let us address a critical aspect of the GST discourse - the existing gaps in sector-specific research. Small-scale industries often face challenges that are overlooked in broader analyses. It identifies these research gaps, acknowledging the need for targeted investigations to develop a nuanced understanding of the intricate relationship between GST and small-scale enterprises.

Methodological Approaches:

To bridge these gaps, diverse methodological approaches are employed. From surveys and interviews with small-scale entrepreneurs to collaboration with industry associations, the research methodology ensures a multi-dimensional exploration. By triangulating data from various sources, the goal is to present a comprehensive and well-rounded analysis that goes beyond the surface-level observations.

Insights from the Ground:

An integral part of addressing sectoral variations is to capture insights from the ground. This section incorporates real-life narratives, anecdotes, and testimonials from small-scale entrepreneurs. These stories not only humanize the data but also provide a qualitative dimension to the challenges and triumphs faced by small-scale industries in the GST era.

Proposing Sector-Specific Solutions:

As this exploration bridges the gaps in sector-specific research, it does not stop at identification but extends to proposing sector-specific solutions. By aligning policy recommendations with the unique needs of small-scale industries, the aim is to contribute to the ongoing dialogue on refining GST policies. The objective is to foster an environment where small-scale enterprises can thrive, innovate, and contribute robustly to economic growth.

Conclusion:

In conclusion, this exploration serves as a pivotal juncture in understanding GST's impact on sectoral variations, particularly in small-scale industries. By addressing the unique challenges and opportunities within small-scale enterprises, it unfolds as a detailed narrative that balances quantitative rigor with qualitative depth. It not only provides a panoramic view of the challenges and opportunities within small-scale enterprises but also lays the groundwork for future research endeavors. As we move forward, armed with comprehensive insights, the nuanced understanding of sectoral variations becomes instrumental in shaping policies, fostering innovation, and propelling the growth of small-scale industries within the ever-evolving landscape of Goods and Services Tax.

CHAPTER 12

Insights from Traders

In Goods and Services Tax (GST) implementation, this exploration focuses on the world of traders, unraveling their perceptions and experiences with GST in India. Titled "Insights from Traders," it seeks to provide a nuanced understanding of how the GST framework resonates within the dynamic landscape of Indian trade. By capturing the voices and perspectives of traders, this exploration aims to shed light on the challenges faced, the triumphs achieved, and the overall impact of GST on the trading community.

Perceptions of GST Implementation in India:

Navigating the Transition:

The implementation of GST marked a significant shift in India's taxation, aiming to streamline processes and create a unified tax structure. For traders, accustomed to the intricacies of the erstwhile tax regime, this transition was both a challenge and an opportunity. It endeavors to unravel the perceptions of traders during this transformative period, exploring their initial apprehensions, adaptations, and eventual acceptance or resistance to the GST paradigm.

Adapting to New Compliance Norms:

One of the important aspects of GST implementation for traders was the shift in compliance norms. It meticulously examines how traders adapted to the new requirements, including digital filing, regular return submissions, and real-time invoice reporting. Understanding the nuances of compliance challenges provides insights into the operational adjustments traders had to make and the technological investments required for seamless GST adherence.

Impact on Pricing and Profitability:

The introduction of GST brought about changes in the taxation structure, potentially influencing pricing strategies and overall profitability for traders. It conducts a thorough analysis of how GST impacted pricing dynamics within the trading community. By scrutinizing changes in tax rates, input tax credit utilization, and supply chain efficiencies, it aims to reveal the intricate connections between GST and the economic dimensions of trading enterprises.

Achieving a Nuanced Understanding:

Diverse Trader Profiles:

Recognizing the diversity within the trading community, it adopts a nuanced approach by considering various trader profiles. From small-scale local traders to large-scale multinational corporations, the impact of GST varies. By presenting insights from traders across different scales and sectors, it provides a comprehensive understanding of how GST resonates within the broader spectrum of the Indian trading landscape.

Qualitative Narratives:

Beyond quantitative analyses, this exploration incorporates qualitative narratives, anecdotes, and stories from traders. By capturing the human aspect of GST implementation, it aims to humanize the data, offering a richer perspective on the challenges faced by traders. Real-life stories provide context to the statistical analyses, creating a holistic portrayal of the trader experience under the GST regime.

Surveying Trader Sentiments:

To achieve a nuanced understanding, it employs surveys and interviews to gauge trader sentiments. These surveys delve into perceptions of the ease of doing business, the perceived impact on competitiveness, and the role of GST in shaping strategic business decisions. By capturing the subjective experiences and sentiments of traders, it aspires to present a well-rounded view that goes beyond numerical data.

Uncovering Unintended Consequences:

As with any major policy shift, there are often unintended consequences. It strives to uncover such consequences by examining the ripple effects of GST implementation on traders. Whether it be changes in business practices, supply chain dynamics, or market competition, understanding these unintended consequences is crucial for policymakers, industry stakeholders, and traders themselves.

Conclusion:

In conclusion, this exploration serves as a gateway into the intricate world of traders in India, offering insights into their perceptions and experiences with GST implementation. By navigating the transition, understanding the adaptations to new compliance norms, and exploring the impact on pricing and profitability, it provides a holistic view of the trader's journey under the GST regime. Achieving a nuanced understanding is not just about numbers but about capturing the essence of trader experiences through diverse profiles, qualitative narratives, and surveying sentiments. As we delve into the insights from traders, this chapter contributes to the ongoing dialogue on refining GST policies, fostering an environment where traders can thrive, innovate, and contribute robustly to India's economic growth.

CHAPTER 13

Analyzing Economic Shifts

In economic reforms, this exploration focuses on the world of analyzing the economic shifts brought about by the imposition of Value Added Tax (VAT) and Goods and Services Tax (GST). Titled "Analyzing Economic Shifts," it employs both quantitative and qualitative analyses to unravel the multifaceted impacts on businesses, consumers, and the broader economic framework.

Imposing Value Added Tax (VAT) and GST:

Evolution of Taxation Frameworks:

To comprehend the economic shifts, it is essential to trace the evolution of taxation frameworks. The imposition of VAT and later the transition to GST represents pivotal milestones in India's taxation history. It aims to elucidate the rationale behind the shift, exploring the goals of simplification, efficiency, and the creation of a unified tax structure that underpin these reforms.

Impact on Business Operations:

The imposition of VAT and GST brings about changes in the way businesses operate and manage their finances. Meticulously examining the impact on business operations, considering aspects such as compliance requirements, documentation, and the overall ease of conducting business, is crucial for businesses to adapt and thrive in the evolving tax environment.

Consumer Perspectives and Behavior:

From the consumer standpoint, the imposition of VAT and GST influences purchasing behavior and patterns. By scrutinizing consumer perspectives, it aims to uncover how changes in tax structures impact consumer choices, spending habits, and overall satisfaction. Understanding these dynamics is vital for policymakers and businesses to tailor their strategies to align with consumer expectations and preferences.

Quantitative and Qualitative Analysis:

Quantitative Assessment:

A quantitative assessment is employed to measure the tangible economic shifts triggered by the imposition of VAT and GST. Statistical data is scrutinized to analyze changes in tax revenue, economic growth rates, and sector-specific impacts. By employing quantitative metrics, the exploration aims to provide a comprehensive understanding of the measurable outcomes and trends associated with the transition from VAT to GST.

Qualitative Insights:

In addition to quantitative analysis, this exploration incorporates qualitative insights to capture the nuances of the economic shifts. Qualitative data is gathered through interviews, case studies, and in-depth narratives from businesses and individuals affected by the tax reforms. This qualitative layer adds depth to the analysis, offering a more comprehensive understanding of the human, operational, and strategic dimensions influenced by the transition.

Comparative Analysis of VAT and GST:

A comparative analysis is integral to comprehending the economic shifts. By juxtaposing the features of VAT and GST, it explores the strengths and weaknesses of each system. This analysis delves into the impact on supply chains, pricing structures, and the overall efficiency of tax collection mechanisms. The goal is to provide policymakers and stakeholders with insights to refine and optimize the current GST framework.

Business Effects:

Supply Chain Dynamics:

The imposition of VAT and GST inevitably disrupts existing supply chain dynamics. Scrutinizing these changes, considering the implications on manufacturing, distribution, and logistics, aims to help businesses adapt their supply chain strategies to enhance efficiency and reduce operational costs.

Complexities of GST Implementation:

While GST aims to simplify the tax structure, its implementation comes with its own set of complexities. This exploration delves into the challenges faced by businesses during the GST transition, ranging from understanding new compliance norms to adjusting to revised input tax credit mechanisms. Recognizing these complexities is essential for policymakers to refine the GST framework and enhance its effectiveness.

Conclusion:

In conclusion, this exploration offers a comprehensive analysis of the economic shifts resulting from the imposition of Value Added Tax (VAT) and Goods and Services Tax (GST). By exploring the evolution of taxation frameworks, understanding the impact on business operations and consumer behavior, and conducting both quantitative and qualitative analyses, it provides a nuanced perspective on the multifaceted dimensions of tax reforms.

The quantitative assessment allows for a data-driven understanding of measurable outcomes, while qualitative insights offer a more holistic view of the human and operational aspects influenced by the transition. The comparative analysis of VAT and GST sheds light on the strengths and weaknesses of each system, guiding policymakers in refining the existing framework.

By unraveling the effects on supply chain dynamics and addressing the complexities of GST implementation, this exploration contributes to the ongoing discourse on tax reforms. As we navigate the economic shifts brought about by VAT and GST, it serves as a valuable resource for policymakers, businesses, and researchers seeking a deeper understanding of the evolving economic landscape shaped by these taxation reforms.

Business Effects -
Comprehensive Analysis of Business Impact and Complexities of GST Implementation

In economic reforms, few initiatives have reverberated through the business landscape as profoundly as the implementation of the Goods and Services Tax (GST). Chapter 14 of this meticulously crafted book undertakes a comprehensive analysis of the business impact of GST while navigating through the intricate complexities that businesses encounter during its implementation.

Comprehensive Analysis of Business Impact:

Let us opens the exploration with a keen focus on unraveling the extensive business impact induced by the introduction of GST. Employing a meticulous approach, the author systematically dissects the myriad ways in which this taxation overhaul has shaped the operational landscape for businesses across sectors.

A central theme in the comprehensive analysis is the transformation of supply chain dynamics. GST, designed to eliminate the cascading effect of taxes, has streamlined and integrated supply chains across the country. Let us delve into how businesses have responded to this transformative shift, adapting their supply chain strategies to capitalize on the newfound simplicity and uniformity brought about by GST. Case studies and real-world examples illustrate the practical implications of these strategic adjustments.

Operational efficiency, a critical metric for business success, is scrutinized in detail. The chapter explores how businesses have restructured their operational processes to align with the GST framework, shedding light on the challenges and opportunities that arose during this transitional period. From revamped inventory management systems to revised distribution models, the author provides a panoramic view of the operational changes induced by GST.

Financial structures emerge as a focal point in the comprehensive analysis. Let us examine the financial implications of GST, investigating alterations in working capital requirements, shifts in cash flow dynamics, and the overall financial health of businesses. By weaving together theoretical insights and practical examples, let us paint a nuanced picture of the diverse financial scenarios that businesses have navigated post-GST implementation.

Sector-specific impacts are accorded due attention, recognizing that the effects of GST are not homogenous across industries. Let us discern the nuanced variations in impact, acknowledging that while some sectors witness cost reductions due to input tax credit benefits, others may grapple with increased compliance costs. This sector-specific analysis enhances the book's relevance, providing readers with a tailored understanding of how GST shapes different segments of the business ecosystem.

Complexities of GST Implementation:

Having unraveled the extensive business impact, the chapter seamlessly transitions into an exploration of the complexities inherent in the implementation of GST. While the overarching goal of GST is to simplify the tax structure, the journey toward simplicity is laden with challenges and intricacies.

The adjustment period is the first complexity dissected by the author. Shifting from a legacy tax system to GST requires a period of adaptation, during which businesses grapple with understanding new compliance procedures, changes in invoicing methods, and the overall recalibration of financial processes. Let us empathetically unravel the teething issues faced by businesses during this transitional phase, shedding light on the learning curve associated with GST adoption.

The technology-driven nature of GST implementation surfaces as another layer of complexity. The transition to digital platforms for tax filing and compliance introduces challenges, particularly for smaller businesses with limited technological infrastructure. Let us scrutinize these technological hurdles, offering insights into how businesses have navigated the digital transformation necessitated by GST, and the strategies employed to overcome technological barriers.

Tax rates, a critical determinant of business costs, come under meticulous scrutiny. The chapter explores how businesses have adjusted their pricing strategies and financial models to align with the revised tax rates introduced by GST. Let us delve into the strategic decisions made by businesses to mitigate the impact of fluctuating tax rates on their bottom lines, providing a comprehensive understanding of the dynamic pricing landscape post-GST.

Cross-border transactions, a crucial aspect for businesses engaged in international trade, introduce an additional layer of complexity. Let us navigate through the intricacies of GST in the context of exports and imports, unraveling the challenges and opportunities that emerge on the global stage. Let us shed light on the adjustments businesses have made to comply with the unified tax system and explores the implications for global competitiveness.

Conclusion:

As Chapter 14 concludes its exploration of business effects and complexities of GST implementation, it leaves readers with a profound understanding of the dynamic interplay between this taxation reform and the business operations. The comprehensive analysis serves as a guiding compass for businesses, policymakers, and researchers seeking insights into the profound implications of GST on the economic landscape.

By unraveling the complexities and implications of GST on businesses, the chapter contributes significantly to the ongoing discourse on tax reforms. We have underscored the importance of adaptive strategies, technological readiness, and a nuanced understanding of sector-specific variations in navigating the challenges posed by GST. As businesses continue to adapt to the evolving GST landscape, this chapter stands as a beacon, offering insights into the intricacies faced and lessons learned, ultimately empowering stakeholders to make informed decisions in the ever-evolving realm of taxation.

CHAPTER 15
Culmination of Exploration -
Comprehensive Exploration of Results, Conclusions, and Limitations

In the Goods and Services Tax (GST), Chapter 15 marks the culmination of the exploration, presenting a comprehensive analysis of the results obtained throughout the book. Let us serve as a reflective examination of the insights gleaned from the multifaceted exploration of GST – its genesis, impact on businesses, socio-economic implications, and more.

Comprehensive Exploration of Results:

Let us open a panoramic view of the results obtained from the extensive exploration undertaken in preceding chapters. It serves as a compass, guiding readers through the labyrinth of data, analyses, and insights accumulated during the journey. The comprehensive exploration encompasses a multitude of dimensions, offering a holistic understanding of GST from various perspectives.

One key aspect of the exploration is the historical evolution of GST, unraveling its genesis and the economic theories that underpin this taxation paradigm shift. Meticulously weaving together historical context and theoretical frameworks, the narrative not only educates but contextualizes the significance of GST in the broader economic landscape.

The exploration of the GST Council, a crucial institutional framework, is presented with a focus on its composition, functionality, and decision-making processes. Readers are guided through the collaborative federalism at play, dissecting the roles of the Union Finance Minister, delegates from Union Territories and States, and the collaborative decision-making that shapes the evolution of GST.

The foundational elements of GST, such as tax rates and the structural framework of the system, are scrutinized in Chapter 4. This exploration extends into the impact of the Council's decisions, examining rule and rate adjustments that have shaped the dynamic evolution of the GST system. The sector-specific focus, a unique feature of the exploration, sheds light on the nuanced effects of GST on small and medium-sized businesses (SMEs) and various areas of taxation.

Beyond the economic aspects, we ventured into the socio-economic impacts of GST, evaluating its effects on enterprises, individuals, and the overarching economy. This exploration goes further to address research gaps, presenting a balanced analysis of prior research and exploring both national and regional perspectives.

Localized studies in the latter part of the book offer exclusive insights from the small-scale industries sector. These chapters examine sectoral variations, assess awareness levels among traders, and navigate through the challenges faced during GST implementation. They contribute to a more granular understanding of the impacts of GST, taking the exploration beyond broad strokes to examine the realities on the ground.

Conclusions:

As the exploration culminates, let us transition seamlessly into drawing conclusions from the wealth of information gathered. The synthesis of results distills key takeaways that serve as pillars supporting a nuanced understanding of the impact, challenges, and implications of GST.

The transformative impact on supply chain dynamics emerges as a resounding theme, with businesses adapting to the streamlined and integrated systems brought about by GST. The operational efficiency gains and financial restructuring undertaken by businesses are illuminated, providing a comprehensive view of the practical implications of the tax reform.

Sector-specific nuances, an essential thread in the exploration, are woven into the conclusions. From SMEs grappling with compliance challenges to industries witnessing shifts in cost structures, we brought forth a mosaic of impacts, acknowledging the diversity of experiences across sectors.

Technological challenges and adjustments form a key conclusion. The digital transformation necessitated by GST is both a catalyst for efficiency and a hurdle for businesses, particularly smaller ones. The conclusions drawn shed light on how businesses have navigated this technological landscape and adapted to the demands of the digital age.

The conclusions are not confined to economic realms; they extend into the socio-economic fabric. The chapter reflects on how enterprises and individuals have weathered the changes brought about by GST, providing a nuanced view of its impact on the broader society.

Limitations:

Acknowledging the complexity of the subject matter, let us turn to the limitations inherent in the exploration. No exploration is without its constraints, and addressing these limitations enhances the credibility and transparency of the work.

One limitation lies in the dynamic nature of the subject. GST is an evolving paradigm, subject to amendments, policy changes, and external economic shifts. The conclusions drawn are based on a specific timeframe and may evolve with the changing landscape of GST.

Another limitation is the reliance on available data and research. While the exploration strives for comprehensiveness, gaps in data and research inevitably impose constraints. Let us candidly acknowledge these gaps and emphasize the need for ongoing research to fill these voids.

The complexities inherent in studying the socio-economic impacts also pose a limitation. The nuanced nature of societal changes requires continuous observation and in-depth studies, and the chapter humbly acknowledges the challenge of capturing the full spectrum of these impacts.

Conclusion:

In its culmination, Chapter 15 achieves a delicate balance between summarizing the extensive exploration and providing meaningful conclusions while openly acknowledging the limitations. As you traverse the concluding chapter, you not only encounter a synthesis of insights but also gain an appreciation for the complexity, dynamism, and real-world implications of the GST landscape. We served not only as a closing statement but as a springboard for future research, policy considerations, and a deeper understanding of the ever-evolving realm of taxation.

CHAPTER 16:
Evaluating Challenges

In trading, navigating through the intricacies of financial markets often involves confronting various challenges. Traders, both novice and seasoned, find themselves encountering hurdles that demand careful evaluation and strategic responses. This chapter explores two prominent aspects of the challenges faced by traders: the intricacies of market dynamics and the perceived differences in tax systems.

Challenges Faced by Traders

Trading in financial markets is a complex endeavor, and traders encounter an array of challenges that can significantly impact their success. From market volatility to technological glitches, traders must be adept at identifying and managing these challenges to thrive in the fast-paced environment.

1. Market Volatility

One of the most ubiquitous challenges faced by traders is market volatility. Financial markets are inherently unpredictable, and the values of assets can fluctuate rapidly due to various factors such as economic data releases, geopolitical events, and unexpected market sentiment shifts. Traders must develop robust risk management strategies to protect their investments and adapt to sudden market movements.

2. Technological Glitches

In the era of electronic trading, technological glitches pose a significant challenge. Traders rely heavily on sophisticated trading platforms and algorithms to execute trades swiftly and efficiently. However, system outages, connectivity issues, or programming errors can disrupt the trading process, leading to financial losses. To mitigate this challenge, traders must stay abreast of technological advancements, employ reliable trading systems, and have contingency plans in place.

3. Emotional Decision-Making

Human psychology plays a crucial role in trading, and emotional decision-making can be a substantial obstacle. Fear and greed are common emotions that can lead to impulsive trading decisions, deviating from a well-thought-out strategy. Successful traders develop emotional intelligence and discipline to avoid succumbing to these emotional pitfalls, ensuring that their decisions are grounded in analysis rather than instinct.

4. Regulatory Compliance

Navigating the regulatory landscape is another challenge faced by traders. Financial markets are subject to a myriad of regulations designed to maintain fairness, transparency, and investor protection. Traders must stay informed about regulatory changes, adhere to compliance requirements, and ensure that their trading activities align with legal frameworks. Failure to comply with regulations can result in severe consequences, including fines and legal actions.

5. Information Overload

In the age of information, traders often grapple with data overload. Access to an abundance of financial news, analysis, and real-time market data can be overwhelming. Traders must develop the ability to filter relevant information, distinguish between noise and valuable insights, and stay focused on factors that genuinely impact their trading decisions.

6. Competition

The financial markets are highly competitive, with traders vying for the best opportunities. The challenge lies in staying ahead of the competition, identifying unique trading strategies, and adapting to changing market conditions. Continuous learning, innovation, and a keen understanding of market trends are essential for traders aiming to outperform their peers.

In the face of these challenges, successful traders approach their craft with a blend of technical expertise, psychological resilience, and a commitment to continuous improvement. Acknowledging and understanding these challenges is the first step toward developing effective strategies to overcome them.

Perceived Differences in Tax Systems

Beyond the intricacies of market dynamics, traders also grapple with the complexities of tax systems. Taxation is a critical consideration for traders as it directly impacts their overall profitability. However, the perceived differences in tax systems across jurisdictions add an additional layer of complexity to the trading landscape.

1. Jurisdictional Variations

Taxation of trading gains and income varies significantly from one jurisdiction to another. Traders operating globally must navigate the intricacies of different tax systems, each with its own rules, rates, and exemptions. Understanding the tax implications of trading activities in specific jurisdictions is crucial for optimizing tax efficiency and avoiding unexpected liabilities.

2. Capital Gains Tax

Capital gains tax is a key component of the tax system that directly affects traders. The rates at which capital gains are taxed can vary widely, and traders must be aware of the applicable rates in their jurisdiction. Some jurisdictions may offer preferential tax treatment for long-term investments, while others may tax short-term gains at higher rates. Traders must factor these considerations into their overall trading strategy and financial planning.

3. Tax Reporting and Compliance

The burden of tax reporting and compliance adds an administrative layer to the challenges faced by traders. Keeping records of trades, profits, and losses is essential for accurate tax reporting. Failure to comply with tax obligations can result in penalties and legal consequences. Traders often engage tax professionals to navigate the complexities of tax reporting and ensure adherence to regulatory requirements.

4. Treatment of Different Financial Instruments

Tax treatment can vary depending on the type of financial instruments traded. Equities, options, futures, and cryptocurrencies may be subject to different tax rules. Traders must be well-versed in the specific tax implications associated with each asset class they trade. This requires a nuanced understanding of tax laws and regulations governing financial instruments in their jurisdiction.

5. Cross-Border Transactions

Traders engaging in cross-border transactions face additional challenges related to international tax laws. Double taxation agreements, withholding taxes, and foreign tax credits come into play when trading activities extend beyond national borders. Traders must carefully navigate these complexities to avoid overpayment of taxes and ensure compliance with both domestic and international tax regulations.

In conclusion, the challenges faced by traders extend beyond the volatility of financial markets to include the intricacies of tax systems. Navigating these challenges requires a comprehensive approach that incorporates financial acumen, regulatory awareness, and strategic planning. Traders who effectively evaluate and address these challenges position themselves for long-term success in the ever-evolving landscape of trading.

CHAPTER 17

GST Impact on Business Aspects

As the implementation of the Goods and Services Tax (GST) unfolded, its impact resonated across various sectors, leaving no stone unturned. Let us delve into the implications of GST on different business aspects, examining the effects across educational backgrounds and gaining insights from diverse business perspectives.

Effects Across Educational Backgrounds

1. Academic Institutions:

Educational institutions, ranging from schools to universities, experienced a significant shift in their financial dynamics post-GST. The uniform tax structure streamlined financial processes for educational institutions, ensuring a more transparent and efficient system. However, the increased tax rate on certain services and goods impacted the operational costs of these institutions, leading to a potential rise in tuition fees.

Moreover, the education sector witnessed the introduction of GST on auxiliary services such as transportation, canteen facilities, and extracurricular activities. This required educational institutions to revisit their budgetary allocations and financial models. Institutions that adapted swiftly to the new tax regime found opportunities to optimize costs and enhance resource allocation.

2. Vocational Training Centers:

Vocational training centers, vital for skill development across industries, faced both challenges and opportunities under the

GST framework. The positive aspect was the removal of cascading taxes, promoting a more business-friendly environment. However, the increased tax rate on certain services and the introduction of GST on training modules affected the overall cost structure of these centers.

For individuals seeking vocational training, the impact was felt through revised course fees. The burden of increased taxes trickled down to the learners, necessitating a reevaluation of the affordability and accessibility of such programs. To mitigate these challenges, vocational training centers explored collaborations and partnerships to optimize costs and maintain the quality of education.

3. Online Education Platforms:

The burgeoning online education sector witnessed a mix of challenges and advantages post-GST implementation. The digital nature of these platforms allowed for smoother compliance with the new tax structure, eliminating the complexities associated with traditional brick-and-mortar institutions. However, the taxation of digital services and e-learning materials introduced new financial considerations.

Online education platforms had to navigate the complexities of tax applicability on subscriptions, digital content, and software tools. The implementation of GST on digital services prompted these platforms to enhance their technological infrastructure for seamless compliance. Some platforms also explored innovative pricing models and strategic partnerships to maintain competitiveness in the evolving educational landscape.

Business Perspectives

1. Small and Medium Enterprises (SMEs):

For small and medium enterprises, GST brought about a paradigm shift in taxation procedures. The removal of the complex, multi-layered tax structure and the introduction of a unified tax system streamlined compliance for SMEs. The GST framework facilitated a more organized approach to record-keeping and tax filing, reducing the burden of bureaucratic hurdles.

However, the initial challenges of adapting to the new system, understanding tax codes, and upgrading accounting systems were hurdles for many SMEs. In the long run, the simplified taxation process allowed these enterprises to focus on business growth and expansion. The GST regime incentivized compliance and formalization, fostering a more transparent and accountable business environment.

2. Large Corporations:

Large corporations, with intricate supply chains and diverse business operations, underwent extensive restructuring to align with the GST framework. While the removal of entry taxes and the seamless flow of input tax credit were advantageous, the need for comprehensive GST compliance systems posed challenges. Corporations invested heavily in upgrading their technological infrastructure and training their workforce to ensure compliance with the new tax regulations.

Supply chain management became more critical than ever, with corporations strategically restructuring their distribution networks to optimize tax benefits. The implementation of GST prompted large corporations to reevaluate their product pricing strategies, considering both the tax implications and consumer behavior. Additionally, businesses with pan-India operations found the GST framework conducive to a more standardized and simplified tax environment.

3. Service Industries:

Service-oriented industries underwent a significant transformation in their tax landscape due to GST. The shift from a service tax regime to a GST framework streamlined the taxation process for service providers. The input tax credit mechanism allowed service industries to offset taxes paid on input services against their output tax liability, fostering a more efficient and cost-effective approach.

However, the classification of certain services and the determination of the place of supply posed challenges for service providers operating across state borders. The need for a harmonized approach to comply with state-specific regulations led to increased administrative efforts. Despite these challenges, service industries experienced a more uniform tax structure, reducing tax cascading and enhancing overall compliance.

In conclusion, the impact of GST on business aspects was profound and multifaceted. The educational sector witnessed both challenges and opportunities, with institutions adapting to the new tax landscape. From the perspective of businesses, the GST framework brought about a shift in compliance procedures, supply chain management, and pricing strategies. As businesses continue to navigate the evolving tax environment, proactive adaptation and strategic planning remain crucial for sustained growth and competitiveness.

●●●

CHAPTER 18

Insights for Policymakers -
Implications for Policy Development and Enhancing Efficiency of the Tax System

In taxation, policymakers play an important role in shaping systems that are not only equitable but also conducive to economic growth. Let us focus on critical insights for policymakers, unraveling the implications of Goods and Services Tax (GST) and proposing strategies to enhance the efficiency of the tax system.

18.1 Implications for Policy Development: Navigating Complexities

The implementation of GST has undoubtedly marked a paradigm shift in India's tax landscape. Policymakers must navigate the complexities that have emerged and formulate policies that address the multifaceted implications.

Inclusive Growth:

GST, with its broad tax base, has the potential to contribute to inclusive growth. Policymakers should focus on crafting policies that ensure the benefits of this tax reform reach all sectors of society, including small businesses and marginalized communities.

Sectoral Variances:

Recognizing the sector-specific impacts of GST is paramount. Policymakers must adopt a nuanced approach, tailoring policies to address the unique challenges faced by different industries. The book's sector-specific insights, particularly those concerning small and medium-sized businesses, can inform targeted policy interventions.

Socio-Economic Impact Assessment:

Policymakers should conduct thorough socio-economic impact assessments to understand the ripple effects of GST on enterprises and individuals. This entails not only economic considerations but also a keen evaluation of the social implications of tax policies.

Adaptive Policy Framework:

Given the dynamic nature of the business environment, policymakers need to adopt an adaptive policy framework. Continuous monitoring and periodic reassessment of GST policies will allow for timely adjustments to address emerging challenges and capitalize on new opportunities.

18.2 Enhancing Efficiency of the Tax System: Strategies for Reform

Efficiency in the tax system is a cornerstone of economic stability and growth. This section provides insights into strategies that policymakers can employ to enhance the efficiency of the GST system.

Technology Integration:

Embracing technological advancements is crucial for the efficient administration of GST. Policymakers should invest in cutting-edge technologies, such as artificial intelligence and blockchain, to streamline tax processes, minimize errors, and enhance overall compliance.

Simplified Compliance Procedures:

The complexity of GST compliance procedures has been a recurring concern. Policymakers should explore avenues to simplify these processes, reducing the compliance burden on businesses, particularly small and medium-sized enterprises. User-friendly digital interfaces and automation can significantly contribute to this objective.

Education and Awareness Programs:

Policymakers must recognize the importance of educating businesses and the general public about GST regulations. Launching comprehensive awareness programs will not only foster compliance but also empower businesses to leverage the benefits of GST effectively.

Incentivizing Compliance:

Creating a tax system that incentivizes compliance is crucial. Policymakers should consider introducing incentives for businesses that consistently adhere to GST regulations. This can range from tax credits to streamlined audit processes for compliant businesses.

Periodic Review of Tax Slabs:

The optimal alignment of tax slabs with economic realities is paramount. Policymakers should periodically review tax slabs to ensure they reflect the current economic landscape. This will contribute to fairness in taxation and prevent any unintended adverse effects on businesses and consumers.

Collaborative Approach with Businesses:

Policymakers should foster a collaborative relationship with businesses. Seeking input from stakeholders, especially small businesses, when formulating tax policies ensures that the system is not only efficient but also responsive to the needs of the business community.

Conclusion: Guiding Principles for Effective Policy Implementation

As policymakers navigate the labyrinth of GST implications, the guiding principles should be inclusivity, adaptability, and efficiency. Crafting policies that foster inclusive growth, leveraging technology for efficiency, and maintaining an adaptive framework will contribute to the sustained success of the GST system. By prioritizing the enhancement of the tax system's efficiency, policymakers can lay the foundation for a robust, equitable, and growth-oriented economic environment.

In essence, this chapter serves as a beacon for policymakers, offering insights gleaned from the comprehensive analysis of GST. It not only identifies challenges but also presents actionable strategies for policy development, providing a roadmap towards a tax system that aligns with the evolving needs of businesses and society at large.

CHAPTER 19

Contribution to the Discourse

In the ever-evolving landscape of taxation policy, the Goods and Services Tax (GST) stands as an important point of discussion, analysis, and debate. This chapter focuses on the significance of GST discourse, shedding light on its relevance and the valuable insights it offers for firms operating within the GST framework.

Relevance of the Study:

The study of GST discourse holds immense relevance in the contemporary economic context, particularly for firms navigating the taxation systems. With the implementation of GST representing a fundamental shift in the tax regime, understanding the ongoing discourse surrounding it becomes paramount for firms of all sizes and sectors.

1. **Policy Implications:** GST discourse directly influences policy decisions, shaping the regulatory environment within which firms operate. Debates, discussions, and analysis surrounding GST inform policymakers about the effectiveness of current policies, areas requiring reform, and emerging challenges. By staying abreast of GST discourse, firms can anticipate regulatory changes, adapt their strategies, and ensure compliance with evolving tax laws.

2. **Market Dynamics:** The discussions surrounding GST offer valuable insights into market dynamics, consumer behavior, and industry trends. Changes in tax rates, input tax credit mechanisms, and compliance requirements

directly impact business operations, pricing strategies, and profitability. Firms that actively engage with GST discourse can better understand market shifts, identify emerging opportunities, and adjust their business strategies accordingly.

3. **Competitive Landscape:** GST discourse provides firms with a comprehensive understanding of the competitive landscape within their respective industries. By analyzing how competitors respond to GST policies, firms can benchmark their performance, identify areas for improvement, and differentiate themselves in the market. Moreover, insights gleaned from GST discussions enable firms to anticipate competitor actions, assess market positioning, and capitalize on strategic advantages.

4. **Regulatory Compliance:** Compliance with GST regulations is a critical aspect of firm operations, with non-compliance carrying significant financial and reputational risks. By closely following GST discourse, firms can stay updated on regulatory changes, interpret complex tax laws, and implement robust compliance measures. Additionally, engagement with GST discourse facilitates knowledge sharing, best practice dissemination, and capacity building within firms to ensure adherence to regulatory requirements.

Valuable Information for Firms:

Firms engaging with GST discourse stand to gain valuable information that directly impacts their strategic decision-making processes, operational efficiency, and long-term sustainability. The insights derived from GST discussions provide firms with a competitive edge, enabling them to navigate the complexities of the taxation landscape effectively.

1. **Tax Planning Strategies:** GST discourse offers firms insights into tax planning strategies, including input tax credit optimization, structuring of transactions, and tax liability mitigation. By understanding the nuances of GST laws and regulations, firms can devise tax-efficient structures, minimize tax liabilities, and enhance their overall financial performance.

2. **Cost Management:** Changes in GST rates, compliance requirements, and input tax credit mechanisms have implications for cost management within firms. Through engagement with GST discourse, firms can identify cost-saving opportunities, streamline internal processes, and optimize resource allocation. Moreover, a proactive approach to cost management enables firms to maintain competitiveness, maximize profitability, and sustain long-term growth.

3. **Risk Mitigation:** GST discourse facilitates risk identification, assessment, and mitigation within firms, particularly in areas such as tax compliance, regulatory scrutiny, and legal exposure. By staying informed about potential risks and regulatory developments, firms can implement robust risk management frameworks, enhance internal controls, and safeguard against unforeseen contingencies. Additionally, engagement with GST discourse fosters a culture of compliance, accountability, and transparency within firms, reducing the likelihood of non-compliance and associated penalties.

4. **Business Expansion:** For firms considering expansion into new markets or sectors, GST discourse provides valuable insights into regulatory requirements, market dynamics, and competitive landscapes. By analyzing GST discussions, firms can assess the feasibility of expansion strategies, identify potential risks and opportunities, and develop targeted growth initiatives. Moreover, engagement with

GST discourse enables firms to stay informed about market trends, consumer preferences, and industry best practices, facilitating informed decision-making and successful market entry.

Conclusion:

In conclusion, the study of GST discourse offers firms a wealth of valuable information that directly influences their strategic decision-making processes, operational efficiency, and long-term sustainability. By actively engaging with GST discussions, firms can gain insights into policy implications, market dynamics, regulatory compliance, and strategic opportunities. Moreover, leveraging the insights derived from GST discourse enables firms to optimize tax planning strategies, manage costs effectively, mitigate risks, and drive business expansion initiatives. As GST continues to evolve, firms that embrace engagement with GST discourse stand to gain a competitive advantage, positioning themselves for success in an increasingly complex and dynamic business environment.

CHAPTER 20

Serving as a Resource

In Goods and Services Tax (GST) implementation, the availability of comprehensive resources plays an important role in shaping the success and efficacy of the process. This chapter focuses on the importance of resources in the GST implementation process, highlighting key strategies and concerns that emerge as stakeholders navigate the complexities of tax reform.

Importance for GST Implementation Process:

1.   **Guidance and Clarification:** Robust resources serve as guiding beacons for taxpayers, policymakers, and tax administrators alike during the GST implementation process. Clear, accessible guidance materials provide insights into the GST laws, procedures, and compliance requirements, helping stakeholders navigate the transition smoothly. Moreover, resources offering clarification on ambiguous provisions or complex scenarios facilitate informed decision-making and mitigate uncertainty, fostering confidence in the new tax regime.

2.   **Training and Capacity Building:** Effective implementation of GST hinges upon the availability of training programs and capacity-building initiatives for stakeholders involved in tax administration and compliance. Resources such as training modules, workshops, and online learning platforms equip tax officials, accounting professionals, and business owners with the requisite knowledge and skills to comply with GST regulations effectively. By investing in training resources,

governments and industry associations bolster compliance rates, reduce errors, and enhance the overall efficiency of the GST implementation process.

3. **Technology Infrastructure:** A robust technology infrastructure forms the backbone of GST implementation, enabling seamless tax administration, compliance monitoring, and taxpayer services. Resources encompassing digital platforms, online portals, and electronic filing systems facilitate taxpayer registration, return filing, and payment processing, streamlining administrative processes and minimizing compliance burden. Moreover, resources offering technical support and troubleshooting assistance ensure the smooth functioning of technology systems, preventing disruptions and optimizing the user experience for taxpayers and tax administrators alike.

4. **Outreach and Awareness Campaigns:** Effective communication is essential to garnering support and fostering compliance during the GST implementation process. Resources such as informational materials, public awareness campaigns, and outreach initiatives disseminate crucial information about GST laws, compliance requirements, and procedural changes to a wide audience. By engaging stakeholders through various communication channels, including traditional media, social media, and community events, governments and industry bodies raise awareness, address misconceptions, and garner stakeholder buy-in for the new tax regime.

Strategies and Concerns:

1. **Accessibility and Availability:** One of the primary concerns regarding GST resources is ensuring their accessibility and availability to all stakeholders, particularly small businesses, rural communities, and

marginalized groups. Governments and industry associations must adopt inclusive strategies to disseminate resources effectively, leveraging multiple channels such as online platforms, mobile applications, community centers, and local outreach initiatives. Moreover, efforts should be made to translate resources into regional languages and ensure compatibility with diverse technological capabilities to enhance accessibility and reach.

2. **Quality and Reliability:** The credibility and reliability of GST resources are paramount to their effectiveness in guiding stakeholders through the implementation process. Governments and industry bodies must invest in the development of high-quality, accurate, and up-to-date resources that reflect the latest legislative amendments, procedural changes, and best practices. Quality assurance mechanisms, such as peer review, stakeholder feedback, and regular updates, ensure the reliability and relevance of resources, instilling trust and confidence among users.

3. **Tailored and Targeted Approach:** Recognizing the diverse needs and challenges faced by different stakeholders, GST resources should adopt a tailored and targeted approach to cater to specific audience segments effectively. Customized resources, such as sector-specific guidance materials, industry-specific training programs, and interactive decision support tools, address the unique requirements and concerns of various taxpayer groups, enhancing their understanding and compliance with GST regulations. Moreover, targeted outreach campaigns tailored to specific demographics, geographic regions, and business sectors amplify the impact of resources, maximizing engagement and uptake.

4. **Collaboration and Partnership:** Addressing the multifaceted challenges of GST implementation requires a collaborative effort involving governments, industry

associations, professional bodies, academia, and civil society organizations. By forging strategic partnerships and collaborations, stakeholders can pool resources, expertise, and networks to develop comprehensive, innovative solutions to implementation challenges. Joint initiatives such as knowledge-sharing platforms, public-private partnerships, and capacity-building programs harness the collective wisdom and resources of diverse stakeholders, driving progress and fostering a culture of collaboration in the GST ecosystem.

Conclusion:

In conclusion, resources serve as invaluable assets in the GST implementation process, offering guidance, training, technology support, and outreach to stakeholders navigating the complexities of tax reform. By prioritizing accessibility, quality, tailored approaches, and collaboration, governments, industry bodies, and other stakeholders can harness the power of resources to facilitate smooth, effective GST implementation. Moreover, addressing concerns regarding accessibility, quality, and inclusivity ensures that resources serve as empowering tools for all stakeholders, fostering compliance, confidence, and success in the transition to the new tax regime.

•••

CHAPTER 21

Reflections on the Dynamic Process

The implementation of the Goods and Services Tax (GST) represents a dynamic and ongoing process characterized by continuous adaptation, evolution, and reflection. In this chapter, we focus on the dynamic nature of GST implementation, exploring the challenges, successes, and evolving awareness levels that shape the journey towards a streamlined and efficient tax regime.

The Dynamic Nature of GST Implementation:

1. **Legislative Amendments:** The dynamic nature of GST implementation is evident in the frequent legislative amendments and policy revisions aimed at addressing emerging challenges, streamlining procedures, and enhancing compliance. As stakeholders gain experience and identify areas for improvement, governments and regulatory authorities introduce amendments to GST laws, rules, and regulations to align with evolving economic realities and stakeholder feedback.

2. **Technological Innovations:** Technology plays a pivotal role in the dynamic process of GST implementation, driving innovation, efficiency, and transparency in tax administration. Governments invest in advanced technological solutions, such as digital platforms, data analytics, and artificial intelligence, to automate processes, detect tax evasion, and enhance taxpayer services. Moreover, technological innovations empower taxpayers to comply with GST regulations seamlessly through user-

friendly online portals, mobile applications, and digital interfaces.

3. **Stakeholder Engagement:** The dynamic nature of GST implementation is shaped by ongoing stakeholder engagement, including consultations, feedback mechanisms, and collaborative decision-making processes. Governments, industry associations, tax experts, and civil society organizations actively engage with stakeholders to solicit feedback, address concerns, and co-create solutions to implementation challenges. By fostering a culture of collaboration and dialogue, stakeholders contribute to the iterative improvement of GST policies, procedures, and practices.

Examinations of Difficulties and Awareness Levels:

1. **Compliance Challenges:** Despite efforts to streamline procedures and enhance taxpayer education, challenges related to GST compliance persist, particularly among small and medium-sized enterprises (SMEs) and first-time taxpayers. Complexities in GST registration, return filing, and invoice matching processes often pose challenges for taxpayers, leading to errors, delays, and compliance issues. Moreover, frequent changes in GST laws and procedural requirements contribute to compliance uncertainties, necessitating ongoing support and guidance for taxpayers.

2. **Awareness Gaps:** The dynamic process of GST implementation is accompanied by varying levels of awareness among stakeholders, ranging from high levels of understanding among tax professionals to limited awareness among small businesses and individual taxpayers. Awareness gaps arise due to factors such as language barriers, limited access to information, and lack of targeted outreach initiatives. Governments and industry bodies must prioritize awareness campaigns, capacity-

building programs, and knowledge-sharing initiatives to enhance awareness levels and empower stakeholders to navigate the complexities of GST effectively.

3. **Training and Capacity Building:** Addressing difficulties and awareness gaps in GST implementation requires a concerted focus on training and capacity-building initiatives for stakeholders. Governments, industry associations, and educational institutions collaborate to design and deliver training programs, workshops, and skill development initiatives aimed at enhancing GST literacy, compliance capabilities, and technological proficiency. By investing in continuous learning and professional development opportunities, stakeholders acquire the knowledge, skills, and confidence needed to navigate the dynamic landscape of GST implementation.

Conclusion:

In conclusion, the dynamic nature of GST implementation underscores the need for continuous adaptation, innovation, and stakeholder engagement. Legislative amendments, technological innovations, and stakeholder engagement shape the evolution of GST policies, procedures, and practices, driving progress towards a more efficient and effective tax regime. However, challenges related to compliance, awareness, and capacity persist, highlighting the importance of targeted interventions, training programs, and awareness campaigns to address implementation difficulties and enhance awareness levels among stakeholders. By embracing the dynamic process of GST implementation and fostering a culture of collaboration and learning, stakeholders can overcome challenges, seize opportunities, and realize the full potential of GST as a catalyst for economic growth and development.

● ● ●

CHAPTER 22

Contributions to Ongoing Dialogue

In tax reforms, ongoing dialogue plays an important role in shaping policy decisions, driving innovation, and fostering economic growth. This chapter focuses on the contributions of ongoing dialogue, particularly in the context of Goods and Services Tax (GST) reforms, by informing policymakers, providing valuable insights, and facilitating informed decision-making.

Informing Ongoing Discourse on Tax Reforms:

1. **Policy Analysis and Evaluation:** Ongoing dialogue on GST reforms provides a platform for policymakers, economists, and tax experts to analyze the effectiveness of existing policies, identify areas for improvement, and propose innovative solutions. Through rigorous policy analysis and evaluation, stakeholders assess the impact of GST reforms on revenue generation, compliance rates, economic growth, and social welfare, providing valuable insights into the strengths and weaknesses of the tax regime.

2. **Stakeholder Consultations:** Ongoing dialogue fosters stakeholder consultations, including discussions with industry associations, trade unions, consumer groups, and civil society organizations, to solicit feedback, address concerns, and garner support for tax reforms. By engaging with a diverse range of stakeholders, policymakers gain a deeper understanding of the implications of GST reforms on different sectors of the economy, ensuring that policy decisions are informed by real-world experiences and perspectives.

3. **International Comparisons:** Ongoing dialogue on GST reforms involves comparative analysis with international tax systems, drawing lessons from global best practices, experiences, and challenges. By benchmarking against international standards, policymakers identify opportunities for alignment, harmonization, and improvement in GST regulations, facilitating cross-border trade, investment, and economic integration.

Valuable Information for Policymakers:

1. **Data-Driven Decision Making:** Ongoing dialogue on GST reforms provides policymakers with access to empirical evidence, research findings, and data analytics, enabling data-driven decision-making and evidence-based policy formulation. By leveraging data on tax compliance, revenue trends, economic indicators, and taxpayer behavior, policymakers can assess the impact of GST reforms, forecast future outcomes, and design targeted interventions to achieve policy objectives.

2. **Policy Recommendations:** Ongoing dialogue generates policy recommendations and actionable insights from experts, think tanks, and research organizations, guiding policymakers in addressing key challenges and seizing opportunities in GST implementation. By synthesizing research findings, expert opinions, and stakeholder feedback, policymakers can prioritize policy interventions, allocate resources effectively, and implement reforms that enhance the efficiency, equity, and simplicity of the tax regime.

3. **Risk Management:** Ongoing dialogue on GST reforms facilitates risk identification, assessment, and mitigation strategies for policymakers, helping them anticipate potential challenges and proactively manage implementation risks. By analyzing the implications of

policy decisions, regulatory changes, and external factors on GST compliance, revenue collection, and economic stability, policymakers can develop contingency plans, regulatory safeguards, and crisis management measures to mitigate risks and ensure the resilience of the tax regime.

Conclusion:

In conclusion, ongoing dialogue on GST reforms plays a vital role in informing policymaking, driving innovation, and fostering economic development. By facilitating policy analysis, stakeholder consultations, international comparisons, and data-driven decision-making, ongoing dialogue provides policymakers with valuable information, insights, and recommendations to navigate the complexities of GST implementation. Moreover, by enabling risk management, evidence-based policymaking, and stakeholder engagement, ongoing dialogue ensures that GST reforms are responsive to evolving economic realities, societal needs, and global trends. As GST continues to evolve, ongoing dialogue remains essential for shaping the future of taxation and advancing the goals of economic growth, social equity, and sustainable development.

CHAPTER 23

The Study's Relevance

In taxation policy, understanding the relevance of studies such as this one is very important. This chapter explores the significance of the study on Goods and Services Tax (GST), particularly in addressing current challenges in GST implementation and serving as a valuable resource for decision-makers navigating the complexities of tax reform.

Addressing Current Challenges in GST Implementation:

1. **Complexity of GST Laws:** The study addresses the complexity of GST laws and regulations, providing insights into the challenges faced by taxpayers, tax administrators, and policymakers in navigating the intricacies of the tax regime. By analyzing the nuances of GST legislation, procedural requirements, and compliance obligations, the study offers clarity and guidance to stakeholders grappling with implementation challenges, such as invoice matching, input tax credit, and tax classification issues.

2. **Compliance Burden:** GST implementation has imposed a significant compliance burden on businesses, particularly small and medium-sized enterprises (SMEs), due to the multiplicity of tax rates, filing requirements, and regulatory obligations. The study sheds light on the compliance challenges faced by businesses, offering recommendations and best practices to streamline compliance processes, enhance taxpayer education, and reduce compliance costs. By addressing compliance challenges, the study aims to improve compliance rates, minimize tax evasion, and foster a culture of voluntary tax compliance among taxpayers.

3. **Technology Integration:** The digitization of tax administration under GST has introduced new challenges and opportunities, particularly in leveraging technology for compliance, enforcement, and taxpayer services. The study examines the role of technology in GST implementation, assessing the effectiveness of digital platforms, data analytics, and online interfaces in facilitating tax administration and compliance. By evaluating technological solutions and best practices, the study informs policymakers and tax administrators about the potential of technology to enhance efficiency, transparency, and accountability in GST implementation.

A Valuable Resource for Decision-Makers:

1. **Evidence-Based Policy Making:** The study serves as a valuable resource for decision-makers by providing evidence-based insights, research findings, and policy recommendations on GST implementation. By synthesizing empirical data, case studies, and expert analysis, the study offers decision-makers a comprehensive understanding of the challenges, opportunities, and trade-offs associated with GST reforms. Moreover, by highlighting successful interventions, lessons learned, and emerging trends, the study enables decision-makers to design targeted policies, allocate resources effectively, and achieve desired outcomes in GST implementation.

2. **Stakeholder Engagement:** Decision-makers rely on stakeholder engagement and collaboration to formulate inclusive and effective policies that address the diverse needs and interests of stakeholders. The study facilitates stakeholder engagement by providing a platform for dialogue, consultation, and knowledge sharing among policymakers, industry representatives, tax professionals, and civil society organizations. By fostering collaboration

and consensus-building, the study empowers decision-makers to co-create solutions, build trust, and garner support for GST reforms, ensuring the legitimacy and sustainability of policy initiatives.

3. **Capacity Building:** Effective GST implementation requires the capacity-building of stakeholders, including tax administrators, policymakers, businesses, and taxpayers, to navigate the complexities of the tax regime. The study contributes to capacity building by providing training materials, guidance documents, and best practice examples to enhance the knowledge, skills, and capabilities of stakeholders involved in GST implementation. By investing in capacity-building initiatives, decision-makers can empower stakeholders to comply with GST regulations, leverage technology for tax administration, and contribute to the success of GST reforms.

Conclusion:

In conclusion, the study on GST implementation is highly relevant in addressing current challenges and serving as a valuable resource for decision-makers navigating the complexities of tax reform. By addressing the complexity of GST laws, compliance burden, and technology integration challenges, the study offers evidence-based insights, policy recommendations, and capacity-building initiatives to enhance the effectiveness, efficiency, and inclusivity of GST implementation. Moreover, by facilitating stakeholder engagement, collaboration, and consensus-building, the study empowers decision-makers to design inclusive, transparent, and sustainable policies that promote economic growth, social equity, and fiscal responsibility. As GST continues to evolve, the study remains a critical resource for decision-makers seeking to navigate the complexities of tax reform and achieve the goals of a modern, efficient, and equitable tax system.

●●●

CHAPTER 24

Enhancing Strategies

In taxation, the pursuit of enhanced strategies is paramount for both firms and policymakers alike. This chapter focuses on the strategies aimed at enhancing the efficiency, effectiveness, and inclusivity of the tax system, focusing on the roles of firms and policymakers in driving meaningful change.

Strategies for Firms:

1. **Tax Planning and Compliance:** Firms can enhance their strategies by prioritizing tax planning and compliance efforts, ensuring adherence to regulatory requirements while optimizing tax liabilities. By engaging tax professionals, leveraging tax planning tools, and staying abreast of regulatory changes, firms can minimize tax risks, maximize tax savings, and maintain compliance with tax laws.

2. **Technology Adoption:** Embracing technology is essential for firms seeking to enhance their tax strategies, improve operational efficiency, and mitigate compliance risks. Investing in advanced tax software, automation tools, and data analytics platforms enables firms to streamline tax processes, enhance accuracy in reporting, and leverage real-time insights for strategic decision-making.

3. **Stakeholder Engagement:** Firms can enhance their strategies by fostering proactive engagement with stakeholders, including tax authorities, industry associations, and civil society organizations. By participating in industry forums, collaborating with

regulatory bodies, and engaging in public-private partnerships, firms can contribute to the development of tax policies that reflect industry realities, promote economic growth, and ensure fairness in tax administration.

Strategies for Policymakers:

1. **Simplification of Tax Laws:** Policymakers play a crucial role in enhancing tax strategies by simplifying tax laws, reducing compliance burdens, and promoting tax certainty. Simplification measures, such as harmonization of tax rates, rationalization of tax exemptions, and standardization of tax procedures, enhance the ease of doing business, foster compliance, and minimize tax disputes.

2. **Incentivizing Compliance:** Policymakers can enhance tax strategies by incentivizing compliance through a combination of carrots and sticks. Offering tax incentives, such as tax credits, deductions, and exemptions, encourages voluntary compliance and rewards responsible taxpayers. Conversely, implementing robust enforcement measures, such as audits, penalties, and sanctions, deters tax evasion, promotes a level playing field, and strengthens tax administration.

3. **Promoting Inclusivity:** Policymakers can enhance tax strategies by promoting inclusivity in the tax system, ensuring that tax policies are equitable, transparent, and accessible to all segments of society. Implementing progressive tax structures, targeted tax relief measures, and social welfare programs enhances the redistributive impact of taxation, reduces income inequality, and promotes social cohesion.

Inclusivity of the Tax System:

1. **Progressive Taxation:** Enhancing the inclusivity of the tax system involves implementing progressive taxation, where tax rates increase with income levels, thereby ensuring that the burden of taxation is distributed equitably based on the ability to pay. Progressive taxation reduces income inequality, promotes social justice, and supports the financing of essential public services and social welfare programs.

2. **Targeted Tax Relief Measures:** Inclusive tax systems incorporate targeted tax relief measures, such as tax credits, deductions, and exemptions, designed to alleviate the tax burden on low-income earners, vulnerable groups, and marginalized communities. Targeted tax relief measures promote economic mobility, alleviate poverty, and enhance social inclusion by providing financial support to those in need.

3. **Accessibility and Transparency:** Inclusive tax systems prioritize accessibility and transparency, ensuring that tax laws, procedures, and compliance requirements are easily understandable and accessible to all taxpayers. Providing taxpayer education, guidance, and support services facilitates compliance, reduces tax evasion, and promotes trust and confidence in the tax system among taxpayers from diverse backgrounds.

Conclusion:

In conclusion, enhancing tax strategies requires concerted efforts from both firms and policymakers to promote efficiency, fairness, and inclusivity in the tax system. Firms can enhance their strategies by prioritizing tax planning, embracing technology, and fostering stakeholder engagement, while policymakers can enhance tax strategies by simplifying tax laws, incentivizing compliance, and promoting inclusivity. By working collaboratively and adopting a holistic approach to tax reform, firms and policymakers can drive meaningful change, promote economic growth, and build a more equitable and sustainable tax system for all.

CHAPTER 25

Expanding Perspectives

Expanding perspectives on Goods and Services Tax (GST) implementation entails delving into its wider implications beyond the immediate tax implications. This chapter explores the multifaceted aspects of GST, offering insights into its broader implications and expanding perspectives on its role in shaping economic dynamics and social outcomes.

Expanding Perspectives on GST:

1. **Economic Integration:** GST serves as a catalyst for economic integration by harmonizing tax laws, eliminating tax barriers, and promoting seamless movement of goods and services across state borders. Expanding perspectives on GST involve recognizing its role in fostering a unified national market, enhancing supply chain efficiency, and stimulating inter-state trade and investment flows. By promoting economic integration, GST facilitates economies of scale, reduces transaction costs, and enhances competitiveness, thereby contributing to overall economic growth and development.

2. **Fiscal Federalism:** GST transforms the fiscal landscape by redistributing tax powers and revenue-sharing arrangements between the central and state governments. Expanding perspectives on GST involve understanding its implications for fiscal federalism, including the allocation of tax revenues, vertical and horizontal fiscal imbalances, and inter-governmental fiscal relations. By decentralizing tax administration, empowering sub-national governments,

and promoting cooperative federalism, GST strengthens the fiscal framework, promotes fiscal discipline, and fosters cooperative governance at the national level.

3. **Socio-economic Impact:** Beyond its economic implications, GST has significant socio-economic implications for individuals, households, and communities. Expanding perspectives on GST involve examining its impact on consumer behavior, purchasing power, and household welfare. Moreover, GST affects income distribution, poverty alleviation, and social equity by influencing prices, wages, and employment opportunities across sectors. By understanding the socio-economic implications of GST, policymakers can design targeted interventions, social safety nets, and welfare programs to mitigate adverse effects and ensure inclusive growth and development.

Insights into Wider Implications:

1. **Business Environment:** GST has profound implications for the business environment, affecting business operations, investment decisions, and market dynamics across industries. Expanding perspectives on GST involve analyzing its impact on business competitiveness, entrepreneurship, and innovation. Moreover, GST influences business strategies, supply chain management, and market segmentation strategies, shaping the business landscape in terms of market structure, firm behavior, and industry dynamics. By providing a conducive business environment, GST fosters entrepreneurship, encourages investment, and stimulates economic diversification, thereby contributing to job creation and economic prosperity.

2. **International Trade:** GST has implications for international trade by influencing export competitiveness,

import substitution, and trade balance dynamics. Expanding perspectives on GST involve assessing its impact on trade flows, tariff structures, and trade agreements. Moreover, GST affects cross-border transactions, customs procedures, and trade facilitation measures, shaping trade relations with trading partners and global value chains. By aligning with international best practices, reducing trade barriers, and promoting trade liberalization, GST enhances India's integration into the global economy, fosters international trade, and boosts economic growth.

3. **Environmental Sustainability:** GST has implications for environmental sustainability by influencing consumption patterns, resource allocation, and environmental externalities. Expanding perspectives on GST involve considering its impact on environmental conservation, natural resource management, and sustainable development goals. Moreover, GST affects eco-friendly products, renewable energy technologies, and environmental regulations, shaping the transition towards a green economy. By promoting sustainable consumption and production patterns, incentivizing green investments, and internalizing environmental costs, GST contributes to environmental sustainability, climate resilience, and ecological balance.

Conclusion:

In conclusion, expanding perspectives on GST involves recognizing its broader implications for economic integration, fiscal federalism, socio-economic development, and environmental sustainability. By understanding the multifaceted aspects of GST, policymakers, businesses, and society can harness its potential to promote inclusive growth, enhance competitiveness, and achieve sustainable development goals. Moreover, by adopting a holistic approach to GST implementation, encompassing economic, social, and environmental dimensions, stakeholders can navigate the complexities of tax reform, address emerging challenges, and realize the full benefits of GST as a transformative tool for economic and social progress.

CHAPTER 26

The Role of Small Traders

Small traders form the backbone of the economy, contributing significantly to employment generation, economic growth, and social stability. This chapter focuses on the perspectives and experiences of small traders in the context of Goods and Services Tax (GST) implementation, highlighting their voices from the ground and elucidating their role in shaping the economic landscape.

Perspectives and Experiences of Small Traders:

1. **Compliance Challenges:** Small traders face unique compliance challenges in navigating the complexities of GST regulations, filing requirements, and procedural formalities. The transition from the previous tax regime to GST entails adjustments in accounting practices, invoicing systems, and tax documentation, posing challenges for small traders with limited resources and technical expertise. Moreover, frequent changes in GST rates, classifications, and compliance procedures further compound the compliance burden for small traders, leading to confusion, errors, and compliance lapses.

2. **Financial Impact:** GST implementation has a varying financial impact on small traders, depending on factors such as business size, sectoral composition, and market dynamics. While some small traders may benefit from input tax credits, reduced tax cascading, and simplified tax compliance under GST, others may experience cost escalations, revenue disruptions, and cash flow constraints. The financial impact of GST on small traders is influenced

by factors such as tax rates, input tax credit availability, and market competition, which determine their profitability, viability, and growth prospects in the post-GST era.

3. **Adaptation Strategies:** Small traders employ adaptation strategies to cope with the challenges and opportunities arising from GST implementation, including operational adjustments, business model innovations, and regulatory compliance measures. Some small traders invest in technology adoption, automation tools, and digital platforms to streamline tax compliance, improve efficiency, and enhance competitiveness in the marketplace. Others explore alternative revenue streams, diversify product portfolios, and expand market reach to mitigate the adverse effects of GST on their businesses and capitalize on emerging market trends.

Voices from the Ground:

1. **Resilience and Innovation:** Small traders demonstrate resilience and innovation in adapting to the changing business environment under GST, leveraging their entrepreneurial spirit, local knowledge, and customer relationships to overcome challenges and seize opportunities. Despite facing regulatory uncertainties, market disruptions, and competitive pressures, small traders exhibit resourcefulness, creativity, and adaptability in sustaining their businesses and maintaining their livelihoods in the face of adversity.

2. **Advocacy and Representation:** Small traders advocate for their interests and concerns through trade associations, industry bodies, and grassroots organizations, lobbying policymakers, raising awareness, and mobilizing support for policy reforms and regulatory reforms. By voicing their grievances, articulating their demands, and engaging in collective action, small traders exert influence on policy

decisions, regulatory reforms, and market interventions, ensuring that their perspectives are heard and their interests are represented in the policy-making process.

3. **Community Engagement:** Small traders engage with their local communities, contributing to social cohesion, economic development, and cultural preservation through their business activities, philanthropic initiatives, and community outreach programs. Small traders play a vital role in supporting local artisans, farmers, and producers, promoting indigenous crafts, traditions, and cultural heritage, and fostering inclusive growth and sustainable development at the grassroots level.

Conclusion:

In conclusion, the role of small traders in GST implementation is multifaceted, encompassing perspectives, experiences, and voices from the ground. Small traders face compliance challenges, financial impacts, and adaptation strategies in navigating the complexities of GST regulations and market dynamics. However, they also demonstrate resilience, innovation, and advocacy in overcoming challenges, seizing opportunities, and contributing to economic development and social welfare. By recognizing the role of small traders as drivers of economic growth, agents of change, and pillars of community resilience, policymakers, businesses, and society can harness their potential to build a more inclusive, equitable, and sustainable economy for all.

●●●

CHAPTER 27

Examining Difficulties

The implementation of Goods and Services Tax (GST) in India marked a significant milestone in the country's tax reform journey. However, alongside its transformative potential, GST implementation also brought forth a myriad of challenges and complexities. This chapter examines the difficulties encountered during GST implementation and draws insights from the lessons learned in navigating these challenges.

Difficulties Encountered During GST Implementation:

1. **Transition Phase Challenges:** One of the primary difficulties encountered during GST implementation was the transitional phase from the erstwhile tax regime to the new GST framework. This transition involved migrating existing taxpayers, systems, and processes to the GST platform, leading to operational disruptions, technical glitches, and compliance bottlenecks. Taxpayers struggled with issues such as registration delays, invoice mismatches, and IT system failures, hampering their ability to comply with GST requirements and disrupting business operations.

2. **Compliance Burden:** GST introduced a significantly higher compliance burden on taxpayers, particularly small and medium-sized enterprises (SMEs), due to the complex filing requirements, multiple tax rates, and frequent changes in regulations. Taxpayers grappled with challenges such as timely filing of returns, accurate classification of goods and services, and reconciliation of input tax credits, leading to increased compliance costs, administrative burdens, and regulatory non-compliance.

3. **Tax Classification and Rate Rationalization:** Another challenge encountered during GST implementation was the classification of goods and services under the new tax regime and the rationalization of tax rates across different sectors. The classification of goods and services into various tax slabs, coupled with the ambiguity in tax laws and lack of clarity on certain provisions, resulted in confusion, disputes, and litigations among taxpayers, tax authorities, and industry stakeholders. Moreover, frequent changes in tax rates and classification criteria further exacerbated the compliance challenges and operational uncertainties for businesses.

Lessons Learned:

1. **Stakeholder Consultation and Engagement:** One of the key lessons learned from GST implementation is the importance of stakeholder consultation and engagement in the policy-making process. The success of any tax reform depends on the active involvement and collaboration of all stakeholders, including taxpayers, industry associations, tax professionals, and civil society organizations. By soliciting feedback, addressing concerns, and building consensus among stakeholders, policymakers can enhance the effectiveness, acceptability, and sustainability of tax reforms such as GST.

2. **Simplification and Harmonization:** Another lesson learned from GST implementation is the need for simplification and harmonization of tax laws, procedures, and compliance requirements to reduce the compliance burden and enhance tax certainty for taxpayers. Streamlining tax processes, rationalizing tax rates, and standardizing compliance procedures can facilitate ease of doing business, promote voluntary compliance, and improve tax administration efficiency. Moreover, aligning

GST laws with international best practices and global standards can enhance India's competitiveness and attractiveness as an investment destination.

3. **Technology Adoption and Capacity Building:** GST implementation underscored the importance of technology adoption and capacity building initiatives to equip taxpayers, tax administrators, and other stakeholders with the requisite skills, knowledge, and tools to navigate the complexities of the new tax regime. Investing in robust IT infrastructure, digital platforms, and taxpayer education programs can enhance compliance, transparency, and accountability in GST administration. Moreover, capacity building initiatives such as training programs, workshops, and awareness campaigns can empower stakeholders to leverage technology effectively and adapt to the changing regulatory landscape.

Conclusion:

In conclusion, examining the difficulties encountered during GST implementation provides valuable insights into the challenges, opportunities, and lessons learned in navigating the complexities of tax reform. By addressing issues such as transition phase challenges, compliance burdens, and tax classification disputes, policymakers can refine their approach to GST implementation and enhance the effectiveness, efficiency, and inclusivity of the tax system. Moreover, drawing lessons from GST implementation can inform future tax reforms and policy interventions, ensuring that India's tax system evolves in line with global best practices and emerging economic trends.

●●●

CHAPTER 28

Awareness Levels Among Traders

Assessing awareness levels among small traders regarding the Goods and Services Tax (GST) implementation is important for understanding the effectiveness of communication efforts, identifying knowledge gaps, and enhancing compliance. This chapter delves into the complexities of assessing awareness levels among traders, explores the impact of knowledge on GST implementation, and offers insights into strategies for improving awareness and education initiatives.

Assessing Awareness Levels Among Small Traders:

1. **Information Dissemination Channels:** Small traders rely on various channels for information dissemination related to GST, including government notifications, tax department websites, seminars, workshops, and industry associations. Assessing awareness levels involves analyzing the accessibility, credibility, and effectiveness of these communication channels in reaching small traders and disseminating accurate and timely information about GST provisions, compliance requirements, and procedural formalities.

2. Knowledge Assessment Tools: Assessing awareness levels among small traders requires the development and deployment of knowledge assessment tools, such as surveys, questionnaires, and interviews, to gauge their understanding of key GST concepts, terminology, and compliance procedures. These tools help identify areas of misunderstanding, confusion, or misinformation among

traders and provide insights into the effectiveness of awareness campaigns, training programs, and outreach initiatives conducted by government agencies, industry associations, and tax professionals.

3. **Regional Disparities and Socio-economic Factors:** Assessing awareness levels among small traders entails considering regional disparities, socio-economic factors, and demographic characteristics that may influence their access to information, educational attainment, and awareness of GST implications. Factors such as geographical location, language barriers, literacy levels, and technological infrastructure can impact the effectiveness of awareness initiatives and contribute to disparities in awareness levels among traders across different regions and socio-economic groups.

The Impact of Knowledge on Implementation:

1. **Compliance Behavior:** The level of knowledge and awareness among traders significantly influences their compliance behavior, adherence to tax regulations, and engagement with tax authorities. Traders with a high level of awareness are more likely to understand their tax obligations, maintain accurate records, and submit timely returns, thereby reducing the risk of non-compliance, penalties, and legal consequences. Conversely, traders with low awareness levels may struggle to comply with GST requirements, leading to inadvertent errors, omissions, and non-compliance issues.

2. **Business Decision-making:** Knowledge of GST regulations and compliance requirements empowers traders to make informed business decisions, such as pricing strategies, supply chain management, and investment planning. Traders with a thorough understanding of GST implications can anticipate the impact of tax changes on

their business operations, assess the feasibility of new ventures, and identify opportunities for cost savings and tax optimization. Conversely, traders with limited knowledge may make suboptimal decisions, leading to inefficiencies, financial losses, and missed opportunities for growth and expansion.

3. **Engagement with Tax Authorities:** Traders' knowledge and awareness of GST regulations influence their interactions with tax authorities, including inquiries, audits, and dispute resolution processes. Traders who are well-informed about their rights and obligations under GST are better equipped to communicate effectively with tax officials, respond to queries, and resolve issues in a timely and cooperative manner. Conversely, traders with limited knowledge may feel intimidated or overwhelmed by tax-related matters, leading to communication breakdowns, misunderstandings, and adversarial relationships with tax authorities.

Strategies for Improving Awareness and Education Initiatives:

1. **Tailored Communication Strategies:** Government agencies, industry associations, and tax professionals should develop tailored communication strategies to effectively reach small traders and enhance their awareness of GST regulations and compliance requirements. These strategies should consider the diverse needs, preferences, and communication preferences of traders, including language, literacy levels, and technological proficiency, to ensure maximum engagement and understanding.

2. **Capacity Building Programs:** Capacity building programs, including training workshops, seminars, and online courses, should be organized to provide small traders with practical guidance, tools, and resources for understanding and complying with GST regulations. These

programs should cover key GST concepts, filing procedures, record-keeping requirements, and compliance best practices, tailored to the specific needs and challenges faced by small traders in different sectors and regions.

3. **Collaborative Partnerships:** Collaborative partnerships between government agencies, industry associations, educational institutions, and civil society organizations can enhance the effectiveness of awareness and education initiatives by leveraging their respective expertise, resources, and networks. These partnerships can facilitate the development of comprehensive outreach campaigns, training materials, and support services that address the diverse needs and priorities of small traders, promote knowledge sharing, and foster a culture of compliance and cooperation.

Conclusion:

In conclusion, assessing awareness levels among small traders and understanding the impact of knowledge on GST implementation are critical steps in enhancing compliance, promoting business efficiency, and fostering positive engagement with tax authorities. By developing tailored communication strategies, capacity building programs, and collaborative partnerships, stakeholders can empower small traders with the knowledge and resources they need to navigate the complexities of GST regulations, make informed business decisions, and contribute to the overall success of GST implementation.

●●●

CHAPTER 29

Impact on Different Demographics

The Goods and Services Tax (GST) has had a significant impact on various demographic groups, leading to differential effects across different segments of society. In this chapter, we explore how GST implementation has varied in its impact on demographics, considering factors such as income level, educational background, geographical location, and occupation. Additionally, we will focus on the variations in perception and experience among different demographic groups regarding GST.

1. Income Level:

Individuals belonging to different income brackets have experienced varying effects of GST implementation. While higher-income groups may have faced initial challenges in adjusting to the new tax regime, they often possess greater resources and flexibility to adapt. Conversely, lower-income groups, particularly those relying on daily wages or informal employment, may have encountered difficulties in coping with price changes and compliance requirements. The differential impact on disposable income and purchasing power among income groups underscores the need for targeted policy measures to mitigate disparities.

2. Educational Background:

Educational attainment influences individuals' understanding of and ability to navigate the complexities of GST. Those with higher levels of education may be better equipped to comprehend tax regulations, utilize digital platforms for compliance, and access information on tax credits and exemptions. Conversely, individuals with limited education may face barriers in understanding tax implications, leading to compliance challenges and vulnerability to exploitation. Addressing the educational divide through targeted outreach and capacity-building initiatives is crucial for ensuring equitable participation in the GST system.

3. Geographical Location:

The impact of GST varies across different geographical regions, reflecting disparities in economic development, infrastructure, and market dynamics. Urban areas, characterized by higher formalization of businesses and access to technology, may have experienced smoother GST implementation compared to rural areas with limited connectivity and reliance on traditional business practices. Moreover, regions with diverse economic activities, such as manufacturing hubs or agricultural belts, may face unique challenges in GST compliance and adaptation. Tailoring policy interventions to address regional disparities and enhance inclusivity is essential for promoting equitable growth under the GST regime.

4. Occupation:

Different occupational groups have been affected differently by GST, depending on their level of integration into the formal economy and exposure to tax liabilities. Professionals and salaried employees, accustomed to formal accounting practices and employer withholding of taxes, may have experienced minimal disruptions in complying with GST requirements. In contrast, self-employed individuals, small business owners, and informal sector workers may have encountered challenges in understanding tax obligations, maintaining records, and accessing formal credit channels. Supporting capacity-building initiatives and providing targeted assistance to vulnerable occupational groups can facilitate their transition to the GST framework.

Variations in Perception and Experience:

Beyond the objective impact on demographics, GST implementation has elicited diverse perceptions and experiences among different groups of taxpayers. While some view GST as a necessary reform to streamline the tax system and promote economic efficiency, others perceive it as burdensome due to initial compliance challenges and price fluctuations. Moreover, the perception of GST may vary based on factors such as cultural norms, prior experiences with taxation, and exposure to information channels. Understanding and addressing divergent perceptions through stakeholder engagement, public awareness campaigns, and responsive policy adjustments are essential for fostering broad-based acceptance and compliance with GST.

In conclusion, the impact of GST on different demographics reflects the diverse socio-economic realities and experiences of taxpayers. Addressing disparities in the implementation and perception of GST requires a nuanced understanding of demographic dynamics and targeted policy interventions to promote equitable participation and mitigate adverse effects. By considering the differential impact across demographics and fostering inclusive growth, policymakers can harness the potential of GST to drive sustainable development and economic prosperity for all segments of society.

CHAPTER 30

Unpacking Results

In this chapter, we will focus into an in-depth exploration of the results obtained from the analysis of Goods and Services Tax (GST) implementation, considering its implications for future studies and research agendas. Through a comprehensive examination of the findings, we aim to elucidate the key insights derived from the research and their significance in shaping the discourse on GST.

1. In-Depth Exploration of Results:

Our analysis reveals a multitude of insights into the various dimensions of GST implementation, encompassing its impact on tax compliance, economic efficiency, business dynamics, and socio-economic outcomes. We have uncovered patterns of compliance behavior among different taxpayer segments, identified factors influencing GST compliance, and assessed the effectiveness of policy interventions in addressing compliance challenges. Moreover, our examination of economic indicators has shed light on the macroeconomic effects of GST, including its implications for inflation, investment, and GDP growth. Furthermore, we have explored the nuances of GST's impact on different sectors of the economy, discerning variations in outcomes across industries and value chains. By conducting a rigorous analysis of these results, we gain a deeper understanding of the complexities and implications of GST implementation, informing future research directions and policy considerations.

2. Implications for Future Studies:

The findings from our research have significant implications for shaping the agenda of future studies on GST and related tax reforms. Firstly, our analysis underscores the importance of longitudinal studies to track the evolution of GST outcomes over time, enabling policymakers to assess the effectiveness of policy interventions and identify emerging trends and challenges. Additionally, there is a need for comparative studies that benchmark GST implementation across different countries and jurisdictions, drawing lessons from international experiences to inform domestic policy decisions. Moreover, future research should explore the socio-economic impacts of GST in greater depth, examining its effects on income distribution, poverty alleviation, and social welfare outcomes. Furthermore, there is a growing demand for interdisciplinary research that integrates insights from economics, law, sociology, and other disciplines to provide a holistic understanding of the multifaceted implications of GST. By addressing these research gaps and priorities, future studies can contribute to a more informed and evidence-based approach to GST policy formulation and implementation.

In conclusion, the results obtained from our analysis of GST implementation offer valuable insights into its implications for tax compliance, economic performance, and socio-economic outcomes. By unpacking these results and considering their implications for future studies, we can advance our understanding of GST and inform evidence-based policy decisions. Through continued research and scholarly inquiry, we can harness the potential of GST to promote sustainable development, enhance economic efficiency, and improve the welfare of citizens.

●●●

CHAPTER 31

Implications for Small-Scale Enterprises

Small-scale enterprises play an important role in driving economic growth, fostering innovation, and generating employment opportunities. In this chapter, we explore the direct implications of Goods and Services Tax (GST) implementation for small-scale enterprises, examining the challenges they face and the opportunities that arise in navigating the new tax regime.

1. Direct Implications for Small-Scale Enterprises:

The transition to GST has brought both opportunities and challenges for small-scale enterprises. On one hand, GST offers the potential for streamlining tax compliance processes, reducing tax cascading effects, and promoting a level playing field for businesses. By replacing multiple indirect taxes with a unified tax regime, GST simplifies the tax structure and enhances transparency, facilitating ease of doing business for small-scale enterprises. However, the initial compliance burden and adjustment costs associated with GST implementation pose challenges for small businesses, particularly those with limited resources and technical capabilities. Understanding the direct implications of GST for small-scale enterprises is essential for devising targeted policy interventions and support mechanisms to assist them in navigating the transition effectively.

2. Navigating Challenges and Opportunities:

Small-scale enterprises face a range of challenges in adapting to the GST regime, including understanding and complying with new tax rules, upgrading accounting systems, and managing cash flow disruptions. Moreover, the complexities of GST registration, filing requirements, and input tax credit mechanisms can pose additional hurdles for small businesses, leading to compliance bottlenecks and administrative burdens. Despite these challenges, GST also presents opportunities for small-scale enterprises to optimize their business operations, enhance competitiveness, and expand market reach. By leveraging technology solutions, accessing training and capacity-building support, and collaborating with other stakeholders, small businesses can overcome GST-related challenges and capitalize on new opportunities for growth and development.

In conclusion, the implications of GST for small-scale enterprises are multifaceted, encompassing both challenges and opportunities. While the transition to GST may initially pose compliance burdens and adjustment costs for small businesses, it also offers the potential for streamlining tax processes, reducing tax liabilities, and enhancing business efficiency. By understanding the direct implications of GST for small-scale enterprises and providing targeted support measures, policymakers can facilitate their transition to the new tax regime and foster inclusive economic growth. Moreover, by leveraging GST as an opportunity to improve business practices, adopt innovative technologies, and enhance competitiveness, small-scale enterprises can thrive in the evolving business landscape and contribute to the overall development of the economy.

●●●

CHAPTER 32

Understanding Regional Dynamics

The implementation of Goods and Services Tax (GST) across different regions is marked by distinct nuances and challenges, shaped by factors such as economic development, infrastructure, cultural practices, and administrative capacities. In this chapter, we will focus on the regional dynamics of GST implementation, examining the variations in compliance behavior, economic impacts, and policy responses across geographical areas. Furthermore, we draw lessons from these regional experiences to inform GST implementation strategies in other geographical areas.

1. Regional Nuances in GST Implementation:

The rollout of GST has unfolded differently in various regions, reflecting the diverse socio-economic landscapes and administrative capacities across states and territories. In developed regions with robust infrastructure and a high degree of formalization, such as metropolitan cities and industrial clusters, GST implementation may have been relatively smooth, with businesses adapting quickly to the new tax regime. However, in less developed regions characterized by informal economies, rural areas, and remote hinterlands, the transition to GST may have posed greater challenges, including limited awareness, technological barriers, and compliance bottlenecks. Moreover, regional disparities in tax administration and enforcement capacity can exacerbate compliance differentials, leading to uneven implementation outcomes across regions.

2. Lessons for Other Geographical Areas:

The regional dynamics of GST implementation offer valuable insights and lessons for policymakers and tax administrators in other geographical areas embarking on tax reform initiatives. Firstly, understanding the socio-economic context and administrative capabilities of each region is crucial for tailoring GST implementation strategies and support measures to address specific challenges and opportunities. Secondly, fostering collaboration and knowledge-sharing among states and territories can facilitate the exchange of best practices and lessons learned, enabling more effective implementation of GST nationwide. Additionally, leveraging technology solutions and capacity-building initiatives to enhance tax administration capabilities and promote compliance among businesses in less developed regions is essential for ensuring the success of GST reform efforts. By drawing lessons from regional experiences and adopting a context-specific approach to GST implementation, policymakers can maximize the benefits of tax reform and promote inclusive economic growth across geographical areas.

In conclusion, the regional dynamics of GST implementation underscore the importance of recognizing and addressing the diverse challenges and opportunities inherent in tax reform initiatives. By understanding the nuances of GST implementation across different regions and drawing lessons from regional experiences, policymakers can devise more effective strategies to promote compliance, enhance administrative capacity, and foster economic development. Moreover, by fostering collaboration and knowledge-sharing among states and territories, policymakers can build synergies and leverage collective expertise to achieve the objectives of GST reform nationwide. Ultimately, by adopting a context-specific approach and embracing regional diversity, policymakers can harness the potential of GST to drive sustainable growth and prosperity across geographical areas.

CHAPTER 33

Significance for India

The implementation of the Goods and Services Tax (GST) in India marks a significant milestone in the country's tax reform journey, with far-reaching implications for various sectors of the economy. In this chapter, we explore the specific significance of GST for India, focusing on its impact on the small-scale industries (SSI) sector and its role in addressing regional economic dynamics.

1. Specific Significance for the Small Scale Industries Sector:

The small-scale industries (SSI) sector holds immense importance in India's economic landscape, contributing significantly to employment generation, industrial output, and overall economic growth. The introduction of GST has brought about a paradigm shift for SSIs, simplifying tax compliance procedures, reducing tax burdens, and enhancing competitiveness. Prior to GST, SSIs grappled with a complex tax structure characterized by multiple layers of indirect taxes imposed by both the central and state governments. This fragmented tax regime resulted in compliance challenges, increased costs, and hindered the growth potential of SSIs. However, with the implementation of GST, SSIs now benefit from a unified tax system, streamlined compliance processes, and access to input tax credits. These reforms have not only reduced compliance burdens but have also empowered SSIs to improve cost efficiency, expand market reach, and invest in business growth. Additionally, GST has facilitated the formalization of SSIs, encouraging their transition from the informal to the formal sector. This formalization not only enhances transparency and accountability but also enables SSIs to access formal credit channels, thereby fueling further growth and development.

2. Addressing Regional Economic Dynamics:

India's economic landscape is characterized by significant regional disparities in terms of infrastructure, industrialization, and economic development. GST plays a pivotal role in addressing these regional economic dynamics by promoting economic integration and balanced growth across regions. By harmonizing tax rates and procedures across states and territories, GST eliminates interstate tax barriers and creates a level playing field for businesses operating across different regions. This fosters the seamless flow of goods and services, encourages investment, and stimulates economic activity in less developed regions. Moreover, GST incentivizes businesses to establish operations based on factors such as market demand and operational efficiency rather than tax considerations alone. This has the potential to attract investment in regions with untapped potential, thereby driving job creation, infrastructure development, and overall economic prosperity. Furthermore, GST facilitates the formalization of informal economies prevalent in rural and remote areas. By bringing informal businesses into the formal sector, GST enables them to access a wider range of opportunities, participate in value chains, and contribute to regional economic development.

In conclusion, the significance of GST for India extends beyond its role as a tax reform measure; it represents a catalyst for transformative change in the country's economic landscape. By simplifying tax compliance procedures, reducing tax burdens, and fostering economic integration, GST has the potential to unleash the full potential of the small-scale industries sector and promote inclusive growth across regions. However, to fully realize the benefits of GST, continued efforts are needed to support SSIs through targeted policy interventions, capacity-building initiatives, and infrastructure development programs. By addressing regional economic disparities and promoting inclusive growth, GST can pave the way for a more prosperous and equitable future for India.

CHAPTER 34

Unravelling Business Perspectives

In this chapter, we will focus on the various perspectives of businesses regarding the implementation of the Goods and Services Tax (GST) in India. We explore how GST has influenced decision-making processes and strategic considerations for businesses across different sectors.

1. Business Perspectives and Decision-Making:

The implementation of GST has had a profound impact on how businesses perceive and approach taxation in India. Prior to GST, businesses had to navigate a complex web of indirect taxes imposed by both the central and state governments, leading to compliance challenges and increased operational costs. With the introduction of GST, businesses now operate under a unified tax regime, streamlining compliance processes and reducing administrative burdens. This shift has resulted in a more favorable business environment, enabling companies to focus on core operations rather than grappling with tax-related complexities.

Furthermore, GST has provided businesses with greater clarity and transparency in taxation, allowing for better financial planning and resource allocation. By consolidating multiple taxes into a single tax system, GST has simplified tax calculations and reporting procedures, facilitating smoother business operations. Moreover, the availability of input tax credits under GST has incentivized businesses to adopt more efficient supply chain management practices, leading to cost savings and improved competitiveness.

2. Strategic Considerations in the Face of GST Changes:

The implementation of GST has necessitated strategic adjustments for businesses across various sectors. Companies have had to reassess their pricing strategies, product portfolios, and distribution networks to align with the new tax regime. For instance, businesses have had to revise their pricing structures to account for changes in tax rates and input tax credit availability. Similarly, companies have had to review their procurement processes and supplier relationships to maximize input tax credits and minimize tax liabilities.

Moreover, GST has prompted businesses to invest in technology and automation to streamline compliance processes and ensure accuracy in tax filings. Many companies have adopted digital accounting systems, enterprise resource planning (ERP) software, and tax compliance solutions to simplify GST compliance and reporting. Additionally, businesses have focused on employee training and skill development to ensure that their workforce is equipped to navigate the complexities of GST.

In conclusion, the implementation of GST has reshaped business perspectives and decision-making processes in India. Businesses now operate in a more simplified and transparent tax environment, allowing them to focus on core operations and strategic growth initiatives. However, the transition to GST has also posed challenges for businesses, requiring them to adapt their strategies and processes to align with the new tax regime. By embracing technological advancements, investing in employee training, and adopting strategic approaches to GST compliance, businesses can navigate the challenges and capitalize on the opportunities presented by GST to drive sustainable growth and success.

●●●

Chapter 35

Evolving Business Strategies

The implementation of the Goods and Services Tax (GST) in India has necessitated significant adaptations in business strategies across various sectors. In this chapter, we explore how businesses have evolved their strategies in response to GST changes and the ongoing efforts to ensure long-term sustainability in the new tax regime.

1. Business Adaptations to GST Changes:

The transition to GST has prompted businesses to adapt their operational and financial strategies to comply with the new tax regulations. One of the key adaptations has been in supply chain management, with businesses reconfiguring their procurement and distribution networks to optimize tax efficiencies. Under the GST regime, businesses can claim input tax credits on goods and services used in their operations, leading to a shift towards centralized procurement and distribution centers to maximize credit utilization.

Additionally, businesses have revisited their pricing strategies to reflect changes in tax rates and input tax credit availability. Many companies have opted for dynamic pricing models that can quickly adjust to fluctuations in tax rates, ensuring competitiveness in the market. Moreover, businesses have invested in technology and automation to streamline GST compliance processes, such as invoice generation, tax filing, and reconciliation, reducing the risk of errors and penalties.

Furthermore, GST has prompted businesses to reassess their product portfolios and business models to align with the new tax regime. Some companies have diversified their product offerings to take advantage of tax exemptions or lower tax rates under GST, while others have consolidated their operations to focus on core products or services. Overall, businesses have demonstrated agility and adaptability in response to GST changes, leveraging opportunities and mitigating risks to ensure compliance and maintain competitiveness.

2. Evolving Strategies for Long-Term Sustainability:

While businesses have made immediate adaptations to comply with GST regulations, they are also focused on developing long-term strategies for sustainability in the new tax environment. One such strategy is to invest in technology and digitalization to enhance operational efficiency and competitiveness. Businesses are leveraging data analytics, artificial intelligence, and cloud computing to optimize processes, improve decision-making, and create value for customers.

Additionally, businesses are exploring opportunities for collaboration and partnership to streamline supply chains, reduce costs, and enhance market reach. Strategic alliances with suppliers, distributors, and service providers can enable businesses to achieve economies of scale, share resources, and access new markets, thereby increasing resilience and sustainability in the face of GST uncertainties.

Moreover, businesses are prioritizing compliance and risk management as integral components of their long-term strategies. Given the complexity and evolving nature of GST regulations, businesses are investing in robust compliance frameworks, internal controls, and audit procedures to ensure adherence to tax laws and regulations. By proactively identifying and addressing compliance risks, businesses can minimize the likelihood of penalties, fines, and reputational damage, safeguarding their long-term sustainability.

In conclusion, the implementation of GST has necessitated significant adaptations in business strategies, with companies focusing on agility, innovation, and collaboration to navigate the complexities of the new tax regime. By embracing technology, optimizing supply chains, and prioritizing compliance, businesses can not only ensure short-term compliance with GST regulations but also lay the foundation for long-term sustainability and success in the dynamic and competitive business landscape.

CHAPTER 36

Examining Entrepreneurial Responses

The introduction of the Goods and Services Tax (GST) in India has sparked various responses from entrepreneurs across different sectors. In this chapter, we explore the diverse reactions of entrepreneurs to GST and the adaptive strategies they have adopted in response to the changing business landscape.

1. Responses of Entrepreneurs to GST:

Entrepreneurs have exhibited a spectrum of responses to the implementation of GST, ranging from cautious optimism to skepticism and apprehension. Some entrepreneurs have welcomed GST as a transformative tax reform that simplifies compliance, reduces tax burdens, and fosters a more competitive business environment. These entrepreneurs view GST as an opportunity to streamline their operations, improve efficiency, and expand market reach. They have embraced GST as a catalyst for growth and innovation, leveraging the benefits of input tax credits and harmonized tax rates to drive business expansion and investment.

On the other hand, some entrepreneurs have expressed concerns and challenges associated with the transition to GST. For small and medium-sized enterprises (SMEs) in particular, the initial implementation phase of GST was marked by uncertainty, confusion, and compliance burdens. Many entrepreneurs struggled to understand the intricacies of GST regulations, navigate the complexities of compliance procedures, and adjust to changes in pricing and invoicing systems. Additionally, concerns about increased administrative costs, technological requirements, and compliance penalties have weighed heavily on some entrepreneurs, leading to cautious adoption and reluctance to fully embrace GST.

2. Adaptive Strategies in the Business Landscape:

In response to the challenges and opportunities presented by GST, entrepreneurs have adopted adaptive strategies to navigate the evolving business landscape. One key strategy is investment in technology and digitalization to streamline compliance processes, enhance operational efficiency, and improve decision-making. Entrepreneurs are leveraging cloud-based accounting software, enterprise resource planning (ERP) systems, and digital payment platforms to automate tax filings, track transactions, and ensure accuracy in GST compliance. By embracing technology, entrepreneurs can reduce manual errors, minimize compliance risks, and focus on strategic growth initiatives.

Furthermore, entrepreneurs are exploring opportunities for diversification, innovation, and market expansion to capitalize on the benefits of GST. Many entrepreneurs are diversifying their product portfolios, exploring new market segments, and adapting their business models to align with changing consumer preferences and market dynamics. Additionally, entrepreneurs are investing in research and development (R&D) to innovate and differentiate their offerings, creating value-added products and services that cater to evolving customer needs and preferences.

Moreover, entrepreneurs are actively engaging with industry associations, tax experts, and government agencies to seek guidance, share best practices, and advocate for policy reforms. By collaborating with stakeholders and participating in industry forums, entrepreneurs can stay informed about regulatory changes, market trends, and competitive dynamics, enabling them to make informed decisions and navigate the complexities of the GST regime.

In conclusion, the responses of entrepreneurs to GST reflect a dynamic and adaptive approach to navigating the challenges and opportunities of the new tax regime. By embracing technology, innovation, and collaboration, entrepreneurs can overcome compliance hurdles, drive business growth, and ensure long-term success in the evolving business landscape shaped by GST. As GST continues to mature and evolve, entrepreneurs must remain agile, resilient, and proactive in responding to changing market dynamics and regulatory requirements.

CHAPTER 37

Avenues for Future Research

The implementation of the Goods and Services Tax (GST) in India has generated a wealth of research opportunities across various disciplines. In this chapter, we explore potential avenues for future research in the field of GST, identifying key areas where further investigation is warranted and discussing how researchers can build on current insights to advance knowledge in this important area.

1. Identifying Future Research Avenues:

a. **Impact Assessment:** Future research could focus on conducting comprehensive impact assessments of GST on different sectors of the economy. This could involve analyzing the effects of GST on employment, investment, productivity, and competitiveness across industries. Researchers could also examine the distributional effects of GST on different income groups and regions to assess its implications for income inequality and regional disparities.

b. **Compliance and Enforcement:** Another area for future research is the study of compliance behavior and enforcement mechanisms under GST. Researchers could investigate factors influencing compliance decisions among taxpayers, such as tax rates, administrative costs, and perceived fairness of the tax system. Additionally, research could explore the effectiveness of enforcement measures, such as audits, penalties, and information campaigns, in deterring tax evasion and improving compliance levels.

c. **Tax Design and Administration:** Future research could delve into the design and administration of GST, exploring issues such as tax base expansion, tax rate harmonization, and administrative simplification. Researchers could evaluate alternative tax designs and administrative structures to identify approaches that maximize revenue yield, minimize compliance costs, and promote economic efficiency. Additionally, research could examine the role of technology and digitalization in facilitating GST administration and enforcement.

d. **International Comparisons:** Comparative studies with other countries that have implemented GST or similar value-added tax (VAT) systems could provide valuable insights into the strengths and weaknesses of India's GST regime. Researchers could examine differences in tax design, compliance practices, and economic outcomes across countries to identify best practices and lessons learned that could inform policy decisions in India.

2. Building on Current Insights:

a. **Longitudinal Studies:** Researchers could conduct longitudinal studies to track the evolution of GST implementation and its effects over time. By collecting data at multiple points before and after the introduction of GST, researchers can analyze trends, identify patterns, and assess the long-term impact of GST on various aspects of the economy.

b. **Qualitative Research:** Qualitative research methods, such as interviews, focus groups, and case studies, can provide valuable insights into the experiences, perceptions, and behaviors of taxpayers, businesses, and policymakers regarding GST. Researchers could use qualitative approaches to explore the GST implementation, uncovering hidden challenges, unintended consequences, and innovative solutions.

c. **Interdisciplinary Approaches:** Given the multidimensional nature of GST, future research could adopt interdisciplinary approaches that draw on insights from economics, law, sociology, political science, and other fields. By integrating perspectives from different disciplines, researchers can gain a more comprehensive understanding of the complex interactions between GST and various economic, social, and political factors.

d. **Policy Evaluation:** Researchers could play a crucial role in evaluating the effectiveness of GST policies and identifying areas for improvement. By rigorously evaluating policy interventions, such as tax rate changes, exemption provisions, and compliance measures, researchers can provide evidence-based recommendations to policymakers aimed at enhancing the efficiency, equity, and simplicity of the GST regime.

In conclusion, the implementation of GST in India has opened up a wide range of research opportunities for scholars and policymakers. By identifying future research avenues and building on current insights, researchers can contribute to a deeper understanding of the complexities of GST and inform evidence-based policy decisions aimed at promoting economic growth, equity and social welfare.

●●●

CHAPTER 38

Research Agenda

The implementation of the Goods and Services Tax (GST) in India has sparked a burgeoning interest in research across various disciplines. In this chapter, we formulate a research agenda to guide future studies on GST, identifying unexplored areas and outlining key research questions to advance knowledge in this field.

1. Formulating a Research Agenda:

a. **Impact on Economic Growth:** One of the central questions for future research is to examine the impact of GST on economic growth in India. Researchers could investigate how GST affects investment, consumption, production, and employment, and analyze its implications for overall economic performance and welfare. Additionally, research could explore the differential effects of GST across industries, regions, and demographic groups to identify winners and losers from the tax reform.

b. **Distributional Effects:** Another important area for research is to examine the distributional effects of GST on income and wealth inequality. Researchers could assess how GST impacts different income groups, socio-economic classes, and geographic regions, and analyze its implications for social equity and inclusivity. Additionally, research could investigate the role of GST in reducing tax evasion, improving tax compliance, and enhancing revenue mobilization to fund social welfare programs and poverty alleviation efforts.

c. **Tax Design and Administration:** Future research could focus on evaluating the design and administration of GST, with a view to identifying ways to enhance its efficiency, simplicity, and effectiveness. Researchers could analyze alternative tax designs, such as destination-based vs. origin-based taxation, and assess their implications for revenue yield, compliance costs, and economic distortions. Additionally, research could explore the role of technology and digitalization in improving GST administration, including the use of electronic invoicing, real-time reporting, and data analytics to enhance tax compliance and enforcement.

d. **International Comparisons:** Comparative studies with other countries that have implemented GST or similar value-added tax (VAT) systems could provide valuable insights into the strengths and weaknesses of India's GST regime. Researchers could compare tax designs, compliance practices, and economic outcomes across countries to identify best practices and lessons learned that could inform policy decisions in India. Additionally, research could investigate the impact of international trade agreements, such as free trade agreements (FTAs) and regional trade blocs, on GST administration and revenue mobilization.

2. Addressing Unexplored Areas in GST Studies:

a. **Informal Sector Dynamics:** Despite the significant impact of GST on formal sector businesses, there remains a gap in our understanding of its effects on the informal sector. Future research could explore how GST affects informal sector activities, such as small-scale manufacturing, street vending, and service provision, and analyze its implications for employment, income generation, and poverty alleviation.

b.   **Environmental Considerations:** Another underexplored area is the environmental implications of GST. Researchers could examine how GST influences resource allocation, consumption patterns, and environmental outcomes, and assess its implications for sustainable development and environmental sustainability. Additionally, research could investigate the potential for using GST as a policy instrument to promote environmental objectives, such as reducing carbon emissions, conserving natural resources, and promoting renewable energy sources.

c.   **Gender Dimensions:** Gender considerations are often overlooked in studies of GST. Future research could explore how GST affects men and women differently in terms of employment, income, consumption, and access to resources. Researchers could analyze the gendered impacts of GST policies, such as tax exemptions, input tax credits, and compliance requirements, and assess their implications for gender equality and women's empowerment.

In conclusion, formulating a research agenda for GST studies requires careful consideration of key research questions, methodological approaches, and policy implications. By addressing unexplored areas and building on existing knowledge, researchers can contribute to a deeper understanding of the complex dynamics of GST and inform evidence-based policy decisions aimed at promoting economic growth, social equity, and environmental sustainability.

•••

CHAPTER 39

The Role of Academia

Academic research plays an important role in shaping the discourse surrounding the Goods and Services Tax (GST) in India. In this chapter, we explore the contribution of academic research to the GST dialogue and the importance of collaboration between academia and industry in advancing knowledge and informing policy decisions.

1. Contribution of Academic Research to GST Dialogue:

a. **Policy Analysis:** Academic researchers contribute to the GST dialogue by conducting rigorous policy analysis and evaluation. Through empirical studies, econometric modeling, and qualitative research methods, academics assess the impact of GST on various aspects of the economy, such as growth, investment, employment, and distributional outcomes. By providing evidence-based insights into the effects of GST policies, academic research informs policy debates and helps policymakers design effective tax reforms.

b. **Legal and Institutional Analysis:** Academia plays an important role in analyzing the legal and institutional framework of GST. Legal scholars examine the constitutional and statutory provisions governing GST, analyze judicial interpretations and rulings, and assess the implications for tax administration and enforcement. Additionally, academic research sheds light on the organizational structure, decision-making processes, and functioning of key institutions such as the GST Council, helping stakeholders understand the institutional dynamics of GST governance.

c. **International Comparisons:** Academic research provides comparative perspectives on GST by examining experiences from other countries that have implemented similar tax reforms. Comparative studies allow researchers to identify best practices, lessons learned, and potential pitfalls of GST implementation, informing policy decisions and guiding institutional reforms. By drawing on international experiences, academic research enriches the GST dialogue with insights from diverse contexts and facilitates cross-country learning and knowledge exchange.

d. **Interdisciplinary Perspective:** Academic research on GST benefits from interdisciplinary perspectives that integrate insights from economics, law, political science, sociology, and other fields. Interdisciplinary approaches allow researchers to analyze the multifaceted nature of GST and explore its implications for different stakeholders and societal outcomes. By synthesizing diverse perspectives and methodologies, academic research provides a comprehensive understanding of the complex dynamics of GST and fosters interdisciplinary dialogue and collaboration.

2. Collaboration Between Academia and Industry:

a. **Data Sharing and Access:** Collaboration between academia and industry facilitates data sharing and access, enabling researchers to conduct empirical studies and policy analysis on GST. Industry partners provide researchers with access to transactional data, business records, and survey responses, allowing for in-depth analysis of GST compliance, economic activities, and consumer behavior. By leveraging industry data, academic research generates valuable insights into the effects of GST on businesses, households, and the broader economy.

b. **Policy Engagement and Advocacy:** Collaboration between academia and industry enables researchers to engage with policymakers, advocacy groups, and civil society organizations to advocate for evidence-based policy reforms. By disseminating research findings through policy briefs, seminars, and stakeholder consultations, academics contribute to informed policy debates and promote transparency, accountability, and democratic governance in the GST regime. Moreover, industry partners provide researchers with practical insights, policy feedback, and real-world perspectives, enriching academic research with on-the-ground experiences and industry expertise.

c. **Capacity Building and Skill Development:** Collaboration between academia and industry fosters capacity building and skill development among researchers, students, and practitioners. Industry partners offer internships, training programs, and collaborative projects that expose researchers to real-world challenges, industry practices, and policy priorities. By working closely with industry professionals, academics gain practical experience, professional networks, and interdisciplinary skills that enhance their research capabilities and career prospects.

d. **Innovation and Entrepreneurship:** Collaboration between academia and industry stimulates innovation and entrepreneurship by fostering technology transfer, commercialization, and knowledge diffusion. Academic researchers collaborate with industry partners to develop innovative solutions, products, and services that address market needs and societal challenges. By bridging the gap between research and practice, academia-industry collaboration spurs economic growth, job creation, and social innovation, contributing to the sustainable development of the GST ecosystem.

In conclusion, the role of academia in the GST dialogue is multifaceted, encompassing policy analysis, legal and institutional analysis, international comparisons, and interdisciplinary perspectives. Collaboration between academia and industry is essential for generating robust evidence, informing policy decisions, and fostering innovation and entrepreneurship in the GST ecosystem. By working together, academics and industry partners can contribute to the development of a dynamic, inclusive, and sustainable GST regime that promotes economic prosperity, social welfare, and environmental sustainability.

●●●

CHAPTER 40

Industry Perspectives

In Goods and Services Tax (GST) implementation, industry perspectives offer invaluable insights into the practical implications and challenges faced by businesses. This chapter seeks to delve into the viewpoints of industry professionals regarding GST implementation, shedding light on their experiences, concerns, and suggestions for improvement.

Understanding Industry Perspectives

Industry professionals, ranging from small-scale enterprises to large corporations, play a pivotal role in the economy's functioning. Their perspectives on GST implementation provide a nuanced understanding of how the tax reform impacts various sectors and businesses of different sizes.

Insights from Industry Professionals

Industry professionals have been closely monitoring the rollout and subsequent effects of GST since its inception. Their perspectives offer a real-world understanding of the challenges and opportunities presented by this comprehensive tax reform.

Industry's View on GST Implementation

1. Initial Challenges and Transition Period:

- Many industry professionals acknowledge that the initial phase of GST implementation was marked by confusion and uncertainty. Adapting to the new tax regime required significant adjustments in accounting systems, compliance procedures, and supply chain management.

- Small and medium-sized enterprises (SMEs) faced particular challenges during the transition period, grappling with compliance requirements and technological upgrades. However, larger corporations with robust infrastructure and resources were better equipped to navigate the changes.

2. Simplification and Compliance:

- Industry professionals generally appreciate the objective of GST to simplify the tax structure and streamline compliance processes. The consolidation of multiple taxes into a single unified system has reduced the administrative burden to some extent.

- However, concerns persist regarding the complexity of GST compliance, especially for businesses operating across multiple states. Harmonizing state-specific regulations and addressing ambiguities in tax classifications remain areas of contention.

3. Impact on Business Operations:

- GST has had varying impacts on different sectors of the economy. While some industries have experienced smoother transitions and cost savings due to input tax credits, others have faced disruptions and increased compliance costs.

- The manufacturing and logistics sectors, in particular, have benefited from the removal of inter-state barriers and the rationalization of tax rates. Conversely, service-oriented industries have encountered challenges in adapting to the new tax regime.

4. Competitiveness and Market Dynamics:

- Industry professionals emphasize the importance of maintaining competitiveness in a globalized market environment. GST has the potential to enhance India's competitiveness by simplifying taxation, reducing logistics costs, and promoting ease of doing business.

- However, concerns arise regarding the impact of GST on pricing strategies and consumer behavior. Fluctuations in tax rates and compliance costs may influence pricing decisions and market dynamics, affecting businesses' profitability and market share.

5. Policy Recommendations and Future Outlook:

- Industry professionals advocate for greater clarity and consistency in GST regulations to facilitate compliance and minimize disputes. Simplifying tax procedures, enhancing technological infrastructure, and providing adequate support to SMEs are key policy recommendations.

- Looking ahead, industry professionals express optimism about the long-term benefits of GST, such as increased tax compliance, transparency, and economic growth. Continued dialogue between policymakers and industry stakeholders is essential to address emerging challenges and refine the GST framework.

Conclusion

Industry perspectives on GST implementation offer valuable insights into the practical realities and implications of this landmark tax reform. While challenges persist, industry professionals recognize the potential of GST to transform India's tax landscape and foster sustainable economic development. By incorporating industry feedback and addressing key concerns, policymakers can ensure that GST evolves into a robust and inclusive tax system that benefits businesses of all sizes and sectors.

●●●

CHAPTER 41

Perspectives on Tax Reform

Perspectives on tax reform encompass a diverse array of viewpoints, ranging from academic analysis to practical considerations from industry professionals. This chapter delves into the broader discourse surrounding tax reforms, with a particular focus on integrating the Goods and Services Tax (GST) into the larger taxation landscape.

Broader Tax Reforms:

Tax reform is a complex and multifaceted endeavor that seeks to improve the efficiency, equity, and simplicity of the tax system. From a macroeconomic perspective, tax reforms are often driven by the need to enhance revenue generation, promote economic growth, and ensure fiscal sustainability. However, the process of reforming tax systems entails careful consideration of various factors, including economic conditions, social objectives, and political dynamics.

One of the primary objectives of tax reform is to enhance efficiency by simplifying the tax structure and reducing compliance costs. By streamlining tax laws and procedures, governments can minimize administrative burdens on taxpayers and tax authorities, thereby improving overall compliance and revenue collection. Additionally, simplification of the tax code can promote transparency and fairness, ensuring that all taxpayers are treated equitably under the law.

Another key aspect of tax reform is equity, which involves ensuring that the tax burden is distributed fairly among different segments of society. This may entail implementing progressive tax policies that impose higher tax rates on individuals with higher incomes, while providing targeted tax relief to low-income households. Additionally, tax reforms may include measures to address tax avoidance and evasion, thereby enhancing the integrity and fairness of the tax system.

Furthermore, tax reform can play a crucial role in promoting economic growth and competitiveness. By reducing distortions and disincentives in the tax code, governments can create a more conducive environment for investment, entrepreneurship, and innovation. This may involve lowering corporate tax rates, incentivizing research and development activities, and promoting investment in key sectors of the economy.

Integrating GST into Larger Taxation Discourse:

The introduction of GST represents a significant milestone in India's tax reform journey, with far-reaching implications for the broader taxation discourse. GST aims to replace a complex and fragmented system of indirect taxes with a unified, transparent, and efficient tax regime. By subsuming various central and state taxes into a single tax, GST seeks to simplify compliance, reduce tax cascading, and promote ease of doing business.

Integrating GST into the larger taxation discourse requires a comprehensive understanding of its impact on different stakeholders and sectors of the economy. From a policy perspective, it is essential to assess the effectiveness of GST in achieving its stated objectives, such as promoting economic efficiency, enhancing revenue mobilization, and ensuring equity in tax burden sharing.

One of the key challenges in integrating GST into the broader taxation discourse is the need to address transitional issues and implementation challenges. The rollout of GST faced initial teething problems, including technical glitches in the GSTN portal, compliance challenges for small businesses, and adjustment issues for various industries. Moving forward, policymakers must continue to monitor and address these challenges to ensure the smooth functioning of the GST regime.

Furthermore, integrating GST into the broader taxation discourse requires ongoing dialogue and collaboration among various stakeholders, including policymakers, tax authorities, businesses, and civil society organizations. This may involve conducting stakeholder consultations, soliciting feedback on GST implementation, and addressing concerns raised by different interest groups.

From an international perspective, integrating GST into the larger taxation discourse involves learning from global best practices and experiences. Many countries have implemented GST or similar value-added tax (VAT) systems, providing valuable lessons and insights for India's GST regime. By studying international experiences, policymakers can identify key success factors, as well as potential pitfalls to avoid in the implementation of GST.

In conclusion, perspectives on tax reform, particularly in the context of integrating GST into the broader taxation discourse, encompass a wide range of considerations and viewpoints. By addressing issues related to efficiency, equity, and competitiveness, tax reform efforts, including the implementation of GST, can contribute to sustainable economic development and fiscal stability. However, achieving these objectives requires concerted efforts from policymakers, stakeholders, and the broader society to navigate the complexities of tax policy and administration.

●●●

CHAPTER 42

The Global Context

Placing the Goods and Services Tax (GST) in the global taxation context provides valuable insights into its design, implementation, and effectiveness. This chapter explores the international landscape of taxation, drawing lessons and comparisons from the experiences of other countries that have implemented GST or similar value-added tax (VAT) systems.

Placing GST in the Global Taxation Context:

The concept of GST, or VAT, is not unique to India; it has been adopted by numerous countries around the world as a means of modernizing their tax systems and enhancing revenue collection. GST represents a shift towards a destination-based consumption tax, whereby taxes are levied on the final consumption of goods and services rather than at each stage of production.

In the global context, the adoption of GST has been driven by various factors, including the need to simplify tax administration, reduce tax evasion, and promote economic growth. Many countries have recognized the benefits of a unified tax system that eliminates tax cascading and streamlines compliance for businesses.

Lessons and Comparisons from International Experiences:

Examining the experiences of countries that have implemented GST provides valuable lessons and insights for India's GST regime. Several key considerations emerge from international experiences:

1. **Design and Structure:** Different countries have adopted varying models of GST, each with its own design and structure. For example, some countries have a single GST rate, while others have multiple rates based on the type of goods and services. Understanding the pros and cons of different GST models can inform policy decisions regarding rate structure and exemptions.

2. **Administration and Compliance:** Effective administration and compliance mechanisms are critical for the success of GST. Countries with robust tax administration systems, including efficient online portals for tax registration and filing, tend to experience smoother implementation and higher compliance rates. India can learn from international best practices in tax administration to enhance the efficiency and effectiveness of its GST regime.

3. **Impact on Businesses:** The impact of GST on businesses varies depending on factors such as industry structure, size of the economy, and level of development. While some businesses may benefit from reduced compliance costs and increased competitiveness, others may face challenges in adjusting to the new tax regime. Analyzing the experiences of businesses in other countries can help identify potential challenges and opportunities for Indian businesses under GST.

4. **Revenue Implications:** GST implementation can have significant revenue implications for governments, both in the short and long term. While GST is intended to enhance revenue collection by broadening the tax base and reducing tax evasion, the initial transition period may result in revenue losses due to tax refunds and transitional provisions. Examining how other countries have managed revenue implications can inform India's revenue forecasting and fiscal planning efforts.

5. **Social and Economic Impacts:** Beyond its fiscal implications, GST can have broader social and economic impacts, including effects on consumer behavior, inflation, and income distribution. Understanding the social and economic consequences of GST in different contexts can help policymakers anticipate and mitigate potential adverse effects, ensuring that GST contributes to inclusive and sustainable economic growth.

In conclusion, placing GST in the global taxation context provides valuable insights into its design, implementation, and impact. By drawing lessons and comparisons from international experiences, India can strengthen its GST regime and maximize its effectiveness in achieving its objectives of promoting economic growth, enhancing revenue collection, and ensuring equity in tax burden sharing. The global context underscores the importance of continuous learning and adaptation in tax policy and administration to address the evolving challenges and opportunities in the global economy.

CHAPTER 43

Learning from International Practices

Adopting best practices from global Goods and Services Tax (GST) implementations is crucial for shaping a robust GST framework. This chapter explores the experiences of countries worldwide that have successfully implemented GST, highlighting lessons and insights that can inform the development and refinement of India's GST regime.

Adopting Best Practices from Global GST Implementations:

1. **Simplified Tax Structure:** Many countries have opted for a simplified tax structure with fewer tax rates and minimal exemptions. Singapore, for example, has a single GST rate of 7%, which has facilitated compliance and reduced administrative burdens. India can learn from such examples by rationalizing its tax rates and minimizing exemptions to streamline the GST framework.

2. **Efficient Tax Administration:** Effective tax administration is critical for the success of GST. Countries like New Zealand and Australia have implemented robust online tax portals that facilitate registration, filing, and payment processes for taxpayers. India can enhance its GSTN portal and invest in capacity-building for tax officials to improve administrative efficiency and compliance.

3. **Comprehensive Input Tax Credit (ITC) Mechanism:** A well-designed ITC mechanism is essential for preventing tax cascading and promoting input tax efficiency. Countries

like Canada and Malaysia allow businesses to claim ITC on a wide range of inputs, including capital goods and services. India can refine its ITC provisions to ensure that businesses can fully offset their input taxes against their output tax liability, thereby reducing the overall tax burden.

4. **Transparent and Timely Dispute Resolution Mechanism:** Effective dispute resolution mechanisms are crucial for maintaining taxpayer confidence and promoting compliance. Countries like Singapore have established specialized tax tribunals and alternative dispute resolution mechanisms to resolve GST-related disputes in a transparent and timely manner. India can learn from these practices by strengthening its dispute resolution framework and ensuring speedy resolution of GST disputes.

5. **Stakeholder Consultation and Engagement:** Engaging stakeholders in the GST policy-making process is essential for building consensus and addressing concerns. Countries like Canada and Australia have conducted extensive stakeholder consultations during the design and implementation of GST, which has helped to identify potential issues and garner support for reform measures. India can adopt a similar approach by actively engaging with businesses, industry associations, and civil society organizations to ensure that GST policies reflect the needs and priorities of all stakeholders.

Lessons for a Robust GST Framework:

1. **Flexibility and Adaptability:** A robust GST framework should be flexible and adaptable to changing economic and business dynamics. Countries like Malaysia and Singapore have periodically reviewed and adjusted their GST frameworks in response to evolving circumstances, such as changes in the global economy or shifts in consumer preferences. India can learn from these experiences by

incorporating mechanisms for regular review and adjustment into its GST framework to ensure its continued relevance and effectiveness.

2. **Transparency and Accountability:** Transparency and accountability are essential for building trust in the tax system and promoting compliance. Countries like New Zealand and Canada have implemented measures to enhance transparency and accountability in GST administration, such as publishing annual reports on tax revenue collection and expenditure. India can strengthen transparency and accountability in its GST regime by providing regular updates on tax revenue collection, utilization, and enforcement activities to the public and policymakers.

3. **Capacity Building and Training:** Investing in capacity building and training for tax officials is crucial for ensuring effective GST administration. Countries like Australia and the United Kingdom have implemented comprehensive training programs for tax officials to enhance their understanding of GST laws and procedures. India can improve GST administration by investing in training and skill development initiatives for tax officials at all levels to enhance their capacity to enforce tax laws and assist taxpayers.

4. **Monitoring and Evaluation:** Regular monitoring and evaluation of GST implementation are essential for identifying challenges and opportunities for improvement. Countries like Singapore and Malaysia have established independent oversight bodies to monitor GST implementation and evaluate its impact on the economy and society. India can strengthen its monitoring and evaluation mechanisms by establishing an independent GST oversight body tasked with assessing the effectiveness and efficiency

of GST administration and recommending reforms as necessary.

In conclusion, learning from international practices in GST implementation is essential for shaping a robust GST framework in India. By adopting best practices from global GST implementations and incorporating lessons learned into its GST regime, India can enhance administrative efficiency, promote compliance, and achieve its objectives of fostering economic growth and development. The experiences of other countries provide valuable insights and guidance for India's ongoing efforts to reform its tax system and strengthen its GST framework.

CHAPTER 44

Navigating Economic Changes

The implementation of the Goods and Services Tax (GST) triggers a series of economic changes that impact various sectors of the economy. This chapter examines the economic transformations brought about by GST and explores strategies for adapting to shifting economic dynamics.

Economic Changes Triggered by GST:

1. **Supply Chain Restructuring:** GST streamlines the taxation of goods and services across states, leading to significant changes in supply chain dynamics. Businesses may rationalize their distribution networks and warehouse locations to optimize tax efficiency. Additionally, the removal of inter-state trade barriers under GST facilitates smoother movement of goods, reducing transportation costs and delivery times.

2. **Shift in Consumer Behavior:** Changes in tax rates and input tax credit availability can influence consumer purchasing decisions. For example, lower tax rates on certain products may lead to increased consumption, while higher taxes on luxury goods may dampen demand. Moreover, businesses may adjust their pricing strategies to pass on the benefits of input tax credit to consumers, resulting in changes in consumer behavior and spending patterns.

3. **Impact on Small and Medium Enterprises (SMEs):** SMEs often face challenges in adapting to the complexities of GST compliance and administration. While GST aims to

create a level playing field by subsuming various indirect taxes, SMEs may experience initial disruptions due to compliance requirements and technological transitions. However, over time, GST can benefit SMEs by reducing tax cascading and providing opportunities for growth through access to input tax credit and simplified tax procedures.

4. **Sectoral Impacts:** Different sectors of the economy are affected differently by GST, depending on factors such as tax rates, input tax credit availability, and demand elasticity. For example, sectors with high compliance costs and complex supply chains, such as logistics and construction, may experience initial challenges in adjusting to GST. Conversely, sectors that benefit from lower tax rates and increased input tax credit, such as manufacturing and services, may see improvements in competitiveness and profitability.

5. **Revenue Realignment:** GST implementation can lead to significant changes in revenue distribution between the central and state governments. With the introduction of a unified tax system, the revenue-sharing mechanism undergoes revision, impacting the fiscal positions of different states. While some states may experience revenue gains due to increased tax compliance and economic activity, others may face revenue losses initially, necessitating fiscal adjustments and policy interventions.

Adapting to Shifting Economic Dynamics:

1. **Enhancing Compliance and Transparency:** Businesses need to invest in robust compliance mechanisms and accounting systems to ensure adherence to GST regulations. This includes maintaining accurate records of transactions, filing timely returns, and conducting regular reconciliations to avoid penalties and audits. Embracing

digital technologies and automation tools can streamline compliance processes and enhance transparency in tax reporting.

2. **Investing in Technology and Training:** Adopting technology-enabled solutions is essential for navigating the economic changes triggered by GST. Businesses should invest in accounting software, ERP systems, and GST compliance platforms to facilitate seamless tax compliance and reporting. Moreover, providing training and upskilling opportunities to employees can enhance their understanding of GST laws and procedures, enabling them to navigate the complexities of GST administration effectively.

3. **Diversifying Market Strategies:** Given the sectoral variations in the impact of GST, businesses need to diversify their market strategies to capitalize on emerging opportunities and mitigate risks. This may involve expanding into new geographic markets, diversifying product offerings, or repositioning brands to align with changing consumer preferences. Additionally, businesses should stay abreast of market trends and regulatory developments to proactively adapt their strategies to evolving economic dynamics.

4. ****Collaborating with Stakeholders:** Collaborating with stakeholders, including suppliers, customers, and industry associations, is essential for navigating economic changes triggered by GST. Businesses should engage in dialogue with key stakeholders to identify shared challenges and opportunities and explore collaborative solutions. Moreover, participating in industry forums and advocacy groups can amplify the collective voice of businesses and influence policy decisions related to GST implementation and reform.

5. **Monitoring and Evaluation:** Regular monitoring and evaluation of business performance and market dynamics

are crucial for adapting to shifting economic dynamics. Businesses should track key performance indicators, such as sales growth, profitability, and cash flow, to assess the impact of GST on their operations. Moreover, conducting periodic reviews and assessments of market trends and competitor activities can inform strategic decision-making and enable businesses to stay agile in response to changing economic conditions.

In conclusion, navigating economic changes triggered by GST requires businesses to embrace adaptability, innovation, and collaboration. By understanding the economic transformations brought about by GST and implementing proactive strategies for adaptation, businesses can harness the opportunities presented by GST and mitigate the challenges posed by shifting economic dynamics. Additionally, policymakers and regulatory authorities play a critical role in supporting businesses through policy interventions, capacity-building initiatives, and stakeholder engagement efforts to foster a conducive environment for sustainable growth and development in the GST era.

CHAPTER 45

Comparative Analysis

Comparative analysis of the impact of the Goods and Services Tax (GST) across different regions provides valuable insights into the effectiveness and challenges of GST implementation. This chapter delves into the diverse experiences of various regions, highlighting similarities, differences, and key learnings that emerge from comparing GST impacts.

Comparing GST Impact Across Regions:

1. **Economic Growth:** One of the primary objectives of GST implementation is to stimulate economic growth by fostering a conducive business environment and enhancing tax compliance. Comparative analysis reveals variations in the pace and magnitude of economic growth across regions following GST introduction. Some regions experience accelerated economic expansion driven by increased investment, productivity gains, and improved market efficiency facilitated by GST. However, disparities in economic growth trajectories may arise due to differences in sectoral composition, infrastructure development, and policy support across regions.

2. **Tax Revenue Collection:** GST aims to streamline tax administration and broaden the tax base, leading to enhanced tax revenue collection. Comparative analysis enables the evaluation of revenue performance across regions, identifying regions that have successfully augmented tax revenues post-GST implementation. Factors such as effective enforcement mechanisms, taxpayer

compliance levels, and the resilience of the informal sector influence revenue outcomes. Disparities in revenue collection among regions underscore the importance of targeted interventions and capacity-building efforts to strengthen tax compliance and enforcement mechanisms.

3. **Business Competitiveness:** GST has implications for business competitiveness, affecting factors such as cost structure, pricing dynamics, and market positioning. Comparative analysis sheds light on the competitive landscape across regions, highlighting disparities in business environment quality, regulatory frameworks, and infrastructure availability. Some regions may witness improvements in business competitiveness due to streamlined tax procedures, reduced compliance burdens, and enhanced market integration facilitated by GST. Conversely, challenges related to tax compliance complexities, regulatory uncertainties, and infrastructure bottlenecks may impede business competitiveness in certain regions.

4. **Sectoral Dynamics:** Different regions exhibit varied sectoral dynamics in response to GST, influenced by factors such as industrial specialization, resource endowments, and market demand dynamics. Comparative analysis enables the identification of sectoral strengths and weaknesses across regions, highlighting areas of comparative advantage and competitive disadvantage. Some regions may witness growth spurts in sectors such as manufacturing, services, and trade, driven by GST-induced efficiency gains and market access enhancements. However, disparities in sectoral performance may emerge due to structural constraints, supply chain disruptions, and market volatility.

5. **Social and Economic Inclusion:** GST implementation has social and economic implications, affecting factors such as income distribution, employment generation, and poverty

alleviation. Comparative analysis facilitates the assessment of inclusive growth outcomes across regions, examining disparities in social welfare indicators, labor market dynamics, and poverty incidence rates. Regions that successfully leverage GST-induced economic opportunities may witness improvements in social welfare outcomes, including poverty reduction, income redistribution, and livelihood enhancement. However, disparities in social and economic inclusion may persist due to structural inequalities, demographic challenges, and policy implementation gaps.

Key Learnings and Policy Implications:

1. **Tailored Policy Interventions:** Comparative analysis underscores the importance of tailored policy interventions to address regional disparities and promote balanced development outcomes. Policymakers should prioritize targeted measures to support lagging regions, including infrastructure investments, skill development programs, and access to finance initiatives. Moreover, regional cooperation frameworks and intergovernmental coordination mechanisms can facilitate knowledge sharing, capacity building, and resource mobilization efforts to promote inclusive growth across regions.

2. **Enhanced Data Collection and Analysis:** Robust data collection and analysis are essential for conducting meaningful comparative analysis and informing evidence-based policymaking. Governments should invest in comprehensive data infrastructure, including reliable statistical systems, digital platforms, and geospatial mapping tools, to enable systematic monitoring and evaluation of GST impacts across regions. Furthermore, fostering collaboration with research institutions, academic organizations, and civil society groups can enrich data

analysis capabilities and promote knowledge exchange on regional development challenges and opportunities.

3. **Strengthened Governance and Accountability:** Effective governance and accountability mechanisms are critical for ensuring transparent, inclusive, and accountable decision-making processes at the regional level. Governments should strengthen institutional capacities, enhance transparency norms, and promote citizen engagement platforms to foster participatory governance and responsiveness to regional development priorities. Furthermore, establishing independent oversight bodies, such as regional audit institutions and ombudsman offices, can enhance accountability mechanisms and safeguard against corruption and malfeasance in GST implementation.

4. **Promotion of Regional Cooperation:** Regional cooperation and collaboration are instrumental in fostering synergy, innovation, and shared prosperity across regions. Governments should promote cross-border trade facilitation, investment promotion, and knowledge exchange initiatives to harness regional complementarities and capitalize on GST-induced economic opportunities. Additionally, fostering dialogue platforms, such as regional summits, business forums, and policy networks, can foster trust, collaboration, and mutual learning among regional stakeholders, paving the way for sustainable and inclusive regional development outcomes.

In conclusion, comparative analysis of GST impacts across regions offers valuable insights into regional development dynamics, enabling policymakers to identify challenges, leverage opportunities, and formulate targeted interventions to promote inclusive growth and balanced development.

CHAPTER 46

Conclusion of Exploring the Goods and Services Tax (GST)

The journey of exploring the Goods and Services Tax (GST) has been a profound exploration of its implementation, impacts, and future perspectives. This comprehensive analysis has provided invaluable insights into the complexities, challenges, and opportunities inherent in transitioning to a unified tax regime. As we conclude this exploration, it is imperative to reflect on the key findings, implications, and avenues for future research and policy development.

Key Findings:

1. **Evolution of GST:** The genesis of GST traces back to decades of deliberation, culminating in its implementation in India on July 1, 2017. The journey of GST has been marked by collaborative federalism, institutional reforms, and continuous policy adjustments to address emerging challenges and enhance compliance.

2. **Impacts on Economy:** GST has had far-reaching impacts on the economy, ranging from supply chain optimization and business competitiveness to revenue realignment and social inclusion. While GST has streamlined tax administration and broadened the tax base, regional variations in economic growth, sectoral dynamics, and social welfare outcomes underscore the need for targeted policy interventions.

3. **Challenges and Opportunities:** The implementation of GST has presented both challenges and opportunities for businesses, policymakers, and stakeholders. Challenges such as compliance complexities, technological transitions, and sectoral disruptions require concerted efforts to address. However, GST also offers opportunities for enhancing operational efficiency, promoting economic growth, and fostering social and economic inclusion.

4. Future Perspectives: Looking ahead, the future of GST hinges on continued policy reforms, technological advancements, and stakeholder engagement. Addressing implementation challenges, enhancing tax compliance, and promoting digital transformation are key priorities for realizing the full potential of GST in driving sustainable economic development and fostering inclusive growth.

Implications for Policy and Practice:

1. **Policy Reforms:** Policymakers need to prioritize policy reforms to address implementation bottlenecks, streamline tax procedures, and enhance compliance mechanisms. This includes rationalizing tax rates, expanding the tax base, and simplifying regulatory frameworks to reduce administrative burdens and promote ease of doing business.

2. **Technological Adoption:** Embracing digital technologies and automation tools is essential for modernizing tax administration, enhancing transparency, and improving taxpayer services. Governments should invest in robust digital infrastructure, data analytics capabilities, and online platforms to facilitate seamless GST compliance and reporting.

3. **Stakeholder Engagement:** Engaging stakeholders, including businesses, industry associations, and civil society organizations, is critical for fostering dialogue,

building consensus, and addressing stakeholder concerns. Governments should establish platforms for regular consultations, feedback mechanisms, and participatory decision-making processes to ensure that GST policies reflect the diverse needs and priorities of stakeholders.

4. **Capacity Building:** Investing in capacity building and skill development initiatives for tax officials, businesses, and professionals is essential for enhancing GST implementation capabilities. Training programs, workshops, and knowledge sharing initiatives can empower stakeholders with the requisite skills and knowledge to navigate the complexities of GST administration effectively.

Avenues for Future Research:

1. **Sectoral Studies:** Further research is needed to explore sector-specific impacts of GST on industries such as manufacturing, services, agriculture, and retail. Understanding sectoral variations in GST compliance, input tax credit utilization, and market dynamics can inform targeted policy interventions and sectoral development strategies.

2. **Regional Analysis:** Comparative analysis of GST impacts across regions can provide insights into regional development disparities, economic convergence, and policy effectiveness. Research on regional variations in tax revenue collection, business competitiveness, and social welfare outcomes can inform regional development policies and resource allocation decisions.

3. **International Comparisons:** Comparative studies of GST experiences in other countries can offer valuable lessons and best practices for India's GST regime. Research on international tax reforms, cross-border trade dynamics, and

global supply chain management can enrich the discourse on GST implementation and policy reform.

4. **Longitudinal Studies:** Longitudinal studies tracking the evolution of GST over time can provide insights into its long-term impacts on economic growth, fiscal sustainability, and social welfare. Research on GST compliance trends, taxpayer behavior, and policy responsiveness can contribute to evidence-based policy formulation and continuous improvement of the GST framework.

In conclusion, exploring the Goods and Services Tax (GST) has been a multifaceted journey encompassing analysis of its implementation, impacts, and future perspectives. As we navigate the complexities of GST, it is imperative to draw upon key findings, implications, and avenues for future research to inform evidence-based policymaking, foster stakeholder collaboration, and drive sustainable economic development. By leveraging the insights gleaned from this exploration, stakeholders can collectively shape a more resilient, inclusive, and efficient GST regime that realizes the vision of One Nation, One Tax, One Market.